PUB ...... from COUNTRY STATIONS

Volume 1

(BEDFORDSHIRE and HERTFORDSHIRE)

Clive Higgs

The Book Castle

First published August 1997
by
The Book Castle
12 Church Street
Dunstable
Bedfordshire LU5 4RU

ISBN 1 871199 53 0

Computer typeset by Keyword, Aldbury, Hertfordshire.
Printed by Antony Rowe Ltd., Chippenham, Wiltshire.

Cover photograph: Sharpenhoe Clappers/Barton Cutting
© Vaughan Basham

CONTENTS

THE AUTHOR

Clive Higgs was born in 1922 in the parish of Mortlake with East Sheen on the extremities of South West London. By 1930 his father had become an avid motorist. Summer Sundays featured the bonus of trips by car to the countryside of South East England, included with which were lavish picnics. Clive soon learned to read maps and became navigator on excursions to places such as The Meon Valley (Hampshire), Christmas Common (on The Chiltern Escarpment in Oxfordshire), Inkpen Beacon (where Berkshire, Hampshire and Wiltshire meet), etc., etc.

Unfortunately for the author the summer of 1935 saw his father's interest in the motor car replaced by the bowling green. Something had to be done to obviate Sundays spent in suburbia. With 2/6d (12½p) in his pocket, donated by his parents, he set off on his first ramble . . . from Boxhill railway station and up into the Surrey Downs at Ranmore Common. Clive has been an ardent rambler ever since, the only interruption being at the time when he served his country in the latter half of World War 2.

He also became a keen cyclist. At no time did the motor car hold any attraction for Clive Higgs, although oddly enough his entire professional career was devoted to the intricacies of vehicle insurance! His extensive knowledge of the highways and byways of South East England are unsurpassed. Even today at the age of 75, Clive regularly goes rambling and with the support of his wife, Anne, hopes to continue to do so for many years to come.

PROLOGUE TO BEDFORDSHIRE

Bedfordshire can be described as a hybrid of the South East and the South Midlands. It is bordered by Hertfordshire, Buckinghamshire, Northamptonshire and Cambridgeshire, the latter forming part of what we used to know as Huntingdonshire. Notwithstanding the fact that much of the county is within a forty minute train journey from Central London, it is for many an unknown quantity. Myriads of people pass through Bedfordshire without even noticing it. They will be speeding down the M1 or the A1(M) on their way to the North or the Midlands, or gliding through at 145mph on an 'Inter City 225' train, *en route* to the North East or Scotland. Patrons of the M1 who may well pause to refresh themselves at 'the Toddington Services' will hardly be aware of the county in which they are pausing. One may regard it as a good bet that fifty percent of them would not opt for 'Beds'!

The county has a low density of population, save for the conurbation of Luton and Dunstable, and the county town of Bedford. Pity it is that the extreme north of the county is inaccessible by rail. For a long time there has been no station between Bedford and Wellingborough in Northants., the lovely remote villages in this region needing to be explored by car, or better still by bicycle. The far south of the region encroaches on the Chiltern Hills. Great are the views across 'the Midland Plain' from such vantage points as Dunstable Downs, Sharpenhoe Clappers and Barton Hills. Luton Airport lies behind the Chiltern Escarpment, its immediate hinterland being an area of narrow lanes and remote farmsteads. The Bedfordshire Ouse is the main drainage channel of the county. This is fed by various tributaries including the little Rivers Flit and Ouzel. The Ouse river pursues a mainly north-easterly direction eventually disporting itself into the sea at The Wash which forms the boundary between Norfolk and Lincolnshire. During its lower course the Ouse traverses the great expanses of the Fenlands. An exception is the River Lea (or Lee) which rises on Leagrave Common near Luton. The Lea goes eastwards and southwards to eventually flow into the Thames in London's East End. Rather a prosaic end to a stream that has traversed such idyllic country in its upper reaches.

Apart from the aforementioned motorways Bedfordshire is 'visited' by the older trunk road system in the form of the A5 and A6. These highways are quieter nowadays as the motorways have absorbed most of the traffic. By train three main lines from London visit the shire on their way northwards. From Kings Cross there are stations at Arlesly, Biggleswade and Sandy. Departing from St. Pancras (or more generally Kings Cross Thameslink nowadays) you can drop off at Luton, Leagrave, Harlington, Flitwick and Bedford itself. The main line from Euston makes a brief incursion into the country at Leighton Buzzard. That completes the points of 'detraining' apart from a few local stations on the Bedford–Bletchley link. Dunstable once had two railway stations, but the link with Luton has been truncated by a new road, making the possibility of revival remote. Now that Mansfield station in Nottinghamshire has been reopened, Dunstable may well currently earn the accolade of the largest town in Britain without a passenger railway.

Mention of the Chiltern uplands has been made. Of the remainder of Bedfordshire it is largely a great plain, save for upland villages situated on 'outcrops' of the Greensand Hills. The further north and east you go, the more the countryside assumes an East Anglian likeness. Wide open spaces abound. Cattle or sheep are scarce; the ground is rich for the growth of crops and fruit. This is not a land which is frequently visited by the rambling fraternity, but local authorities must be congratulated on ensuring that the rights of way are well waymarked . . . a real boon since some of the remote paths would otherwise be difficult to follow. Here's therefore hoping that the selection of five walks in this region afford the reader both peace and enjoyment.

PROLOGUE TO HERTFORDSHIRE

Hertfordshire is bounded by Buckinghamshire, Bedfordshire, Cambridgeshire, Essex and 'Greater London'. It is a county of great contrasts. In the south it impinges upon suburbia in places such as High (or Chipping) Barnet and Bushey, etc. To the east on the boundary with Essex, it assumes an East Anglian flavour with often hedgeless lanes and rich cereal growing acres. In its north west, the county points a finger between the borders of Bucks and Beds. This encompasses a portion of the Vale of Aylesbury, which was described by the poet, Rupert Brooke, as 'the Slumbering Midland Plain'. Within this part of the country, also lies the dormitory town of Tring and the lofty heights around Ivinghoe Beacon.

There are places of size within. Watford, whose town centre has been 'improved' beyond all recognition; Stevenage which used to be a coaching town on the old A1 road has expanded all over the surrounding fields to become an 'overspill town'; and the garden cities of Letchworth and Welwyn. The latter grew up in the thirties ostensibly to become pleasant places in which local workers could spend their lives. Away from these towns there are many square miles of real country, sometimes virtually on the doorsteps of the built-up pieces. Hertfordshire is not a flat county. A large proportion lies within the Chiltern Hills which describe an arc around the London Basin from Goring-on-Thames in Oxfordshire to the bare open downs on the borders of Herts and Cambridgeshire. Within these bounds, woodland is prolific as is also the existence of dry valleys, dry because the chalky soil quickly absorbs the rainfall leaving it to flow underground. There are however a few rivers, the major of which are the Colne and the Lea (or Lee), the latter for a distance forming the boundary with Essex. Minor tributaries of the Colne are the Gade (pronounced Gad) and the Chess, which begins its course at Chesham in Bucks.

Easy access by the motorist from the Metropolis is gained by the A41, A5, A6, and A10 trunk roads, and by the M1 and A1(M) motorways. The railway from Euston serves the Colne and the Gade valleys. West of Watford, the Chiltern Lines and London Underground (Metropolitan) lines link Marylebone and the City respectively. From Brighton, Croydon and Kings Cross (Thameslink) a rail link is available to the City of St. Albans and Harpenden on its way to Bedford, and from Liverpool Street 'WAGN' (West Anglia Great Northern) lines serve the industrial wastes of the lower Lea Valley and the county town of Hertford, which is also served by a branch from the main line from Kings Cross, the latter serving Hatfield, Stevenage, Hitchin, etc. The scene is completed by a somewhat primitive branch line from Watford Junction to St. Albans (Abbey) station.

In short when you go rambling in Hertfordshire, be prepared for a wide variety of terrain and scenery. In the Chiltern area paths are well used and the locality has always been popular for exploration by foot. The nine walks in this book will give the reader an insight into the county as a whole and should prove to be enjoyable to all who treasure and respect the English countryside.

FOREWORD

In the past few years 'pub walk' books have become increasingly popular. Not really surprising as rambling has become the leading outdoor pursuit of those who seek a combination of fresh air and physical fitness. In this particular volume a departure has been made from most others in that the route does not commence at the same pub as where it ends. The concept behind this latest selection of rambles is that the stop for refreshment shall be as near as possible to the halfway point.

The walks start and end at the same railway station. How you make your approach is entirely up to you. Stations nowadays have commodious car parks and although space in them may be at a premium on weekdays, there is plenty of room on Saturdays and Sundays. Alternatively you have the option of going by train. At least if this method of transport is taken then the participants will have no fear of the breathalyser if they partake of a pint or two of the best.

You most probably have noticed how the English country inn has undergone a metamorphosis in the last few years. Gone are the days when a packet of potato crisps or a pickled egg were the only 'solids' to help your ale down. Food and good food too is available in an abundance of choices and mainly at very reasonable prices. It is even rare nowadays to find an establishment that does not cater for special tastes, e.g. vegetarian dishes. Similarly thanks mainly to the efforts of CAMRA (The Campaign for Real Ale) cask beer has now returned to the general scene.

In the main there is no reason why you cannot take the family with you. Most public houses have areas which permit children. Where no such facility exists and when the weather permits, there is always the alternative of the beer garden. A glance at the menu usually reveals that reduced price dishes are available for the 'under twelves'. In addition to non-alcoholic drinks, coffee is now a viable alternative.

The walks vary in distance from 4 to 7¾ miles. Sections along roads have been kept to a minimum. Care has been taken to ensure with the highest degree of accuracy that the 'offroad' sections follow designated rights of way. Even if you are not already skilled in reading a map you are advised to take one with you. You will soon develop the art of translating what you see on the map to the surrounding topographical features. If by any chance you should accidentally stray from the prescribed route and are confronted by the landowner or his agent, humility should be the order of the day. The best approach should be to explain that you have inadvertently strayed from the path, and could we please be directed back to it!

A word about train fares. If you are travelling from most parts of the south-east, you can buy a cheap day return ticket which is available all day on Saturdays, Sundays and Bank Holidays, or after 9.30am on weekdays. As a further economy an annual 'Network Card' can be purchased for a sum of £15. This gives the holder and a second designated partner a 35% discount on rail tickets, but heed the fact that these discounts are not available before 10am on weekdays. Rambling is an all the year pastime, but remember that the English countryside can become decidedly 'tacky' after a wet spell, and in these circumstances something in the way of Wellington boots is to be recommended. The countryside can look idyllic in the Spring or High Summer, and equally attractive in the golden days of Autumn, or the frosts and mists of midwinter. Indeed the author researched one of these pub walks on a day in December, just before Christmastide. Fallen snow was lying on the ground and the hills and woods were shrouded in mist. Navigation was impaired but not difficult. The Hertfordshire countryside resembled Fairyland. The warmth of the pub came as a welcome interlude and amongst the victuals on sale was strongish ale picturesquely entitled 'Santa's Revenge'!

9

WALKS SUMMARY

11

ACCESS BY ROAD

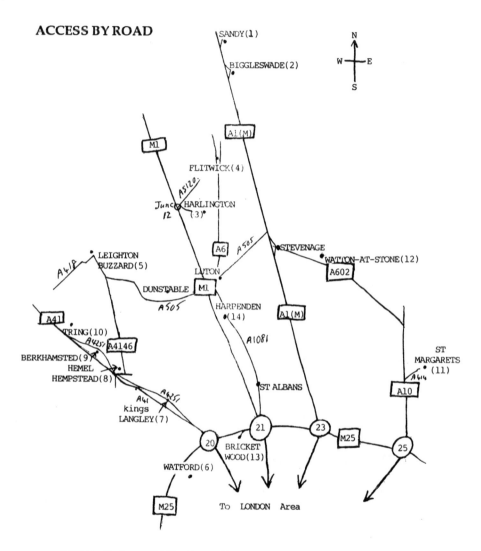

Junction Numbers of M25, thus.. 21

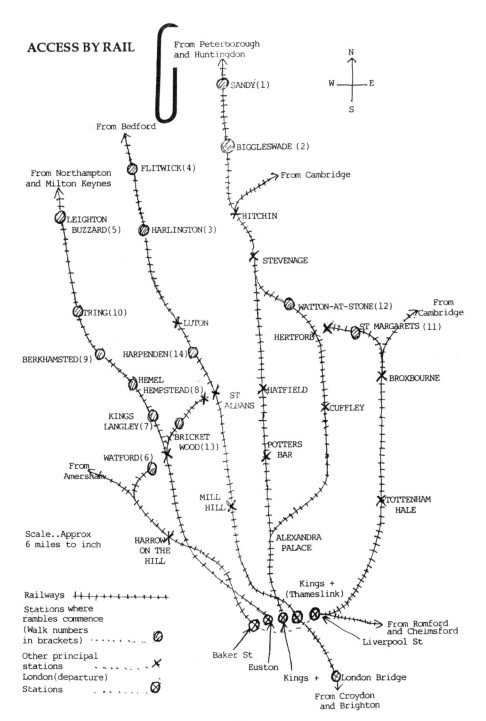

ACCESS BY RAIL

From Peterborough and Huntingdon

N
W — E
S

SANDY(1)

From Bedford

BIGGLESWADE (2)

From Northampton and Milton Keynes

FLITWICK(4)

From Cambridge

LEIGHTON BUZZARD(5)

HARLINGTON(3)

HITCHIN

STEVENAGE

TRING(10)

LUTON

WATTON-AT-STONE(12)

From Cambridge

ST MARGARETS (11)

HERTFORD

BERKHAMSTED(9)

HARPENDEN(14)

BROXBOURNE

HEMEL HEMPSTEAD(8)

ST ALBANS

HATFIELD

CUFFLEY

KINGS LANGLEY(7)

BRICKET WOOD(13)

POTTERS BAR

WATFORD(6)

From Amersham

MILL HILL

TOTTENHAM HALE

Scale..Approx 6 miles to inch

HARROW ON THE HILL

ALEXANDRA PALACE

Kings + (Thameslink)

Railways

Stations where rambles commence (Walk numbers in brackets)

Other principal stations

London(departure) Stations

From Romford and Chelmsford

Liverpool St

Baker St

Euston

Kings +

London Bridge

From Croydon and Brighton

13

THE COUNTRY CODE

1. Avoid damage to fences, gates and walls. These are there for a purpose and to repair damage is often expensive.
2. Always close gates to prevent livestock escaping.
3. Keep to footpaths and other rights of way and avoid causing damage to crops.
4. Respect other people's property. Farm machinery is often left unattended close to where it is needed and should therefore be left untouched.
5. Keep dogs under control and if necessary keep them on a lead. If you cannot control your pet you should not take it out into the countryside. This applies not only where livestock is concerned but to many other areas. Rampaging dogs pose a serious threat to deer, especially when they have young, and desertion and even premature abortion sometimes result. Other wild mammals are disturbed as well as ground-nesting or ground-feeding birds.
6. Do not leave litter and especially do not discard lighted cigarettes, matches or anything else that could start a fire.
7. Drive slowly and safely in the country. Always assume that there might be a herd of cows or a stationary tractor round the next bend.
8. When walking on country roads always remember to keep to the right, in single file.

MUDDY FOOTWEAR

Publicans usually welcome ramblers. Accordingly it is right and proper that muddy shoes or boots should be removed before entry, therefore in the appropriate season it is wise to carry a pair of carpet slippers or plimsolls.

MAP SYMBOLS

Roads ————————

Tracks or Drives — — — — — — — —

Footpaths ·················

Railways ┼┼┼┼┼┼┼┼┼┼┼┼┼

Woods

Walk 1

SANDY TO 'the Thornton Arms', EVERTON and back

BY RAIL . . . West Anglia Great Northern trains from London (Kings Cross) station. Passes *en route* Hatfield, Stevenage and Hitchin, etc. At least one train per hour.

BY ROAD . . . Sandy is just off the A1(M) road. For town centre leave A1(M) via B1042. Station and adjacent car park are at far end of town.

MAP . . . Ordnance Survey Landranger Sheet 153.

DISTANCE OF WALK . . . Approximately 5½ miles.

TOPOGRAPHY . . . This route is in the northerly extremity of Bedfordshire and includes a short but steep rise into an outpost of the Greensand Hills. In the peaceful village of Everton (part of which was once in Huntingdonshire) you will find no football crowds as you would in its namesake on Merseyside! Great views open out to the low lying lands below before you eventually descend among trees back to the starting point. It is a walk for all seasons, but heed should be taken of the fact that the Roman road on the outgoing route can become muddy after rain, particularly in the vicinity of the gates.

SANDY is a smallish but growing town situated on the Great North Road which leads from London to Edinburgh. It also lies on 'the East Coast Main Line' which has a similar destination. The development of the locality has its origins in the fact that there are plenty of 'mile a minute' commuter trains to London. The town in now by-passed and lies to the west of the railway station. Across the railway line and to

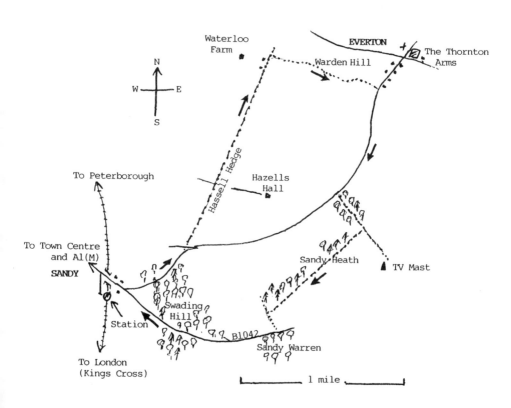

Waterloo Farm

EVERTON

The Thornton Arms

Warden Hill

N
W — E
S

Hassell Hedge

To Peterborough

Hazells Hall

To Town Centre
and A1(M)

SANDY

Sandy Heath

TV Mast

Swading Hill

Station

B1042

Sandy Warren

To London
(Kings Cross)

1 mile

16

the east one is soon in a belt of well-wooded country situated on a low but conspicuous hillside, beyond which are the great plains of Cambridgeshire and beyond these the vast area of the Fenlands. Sandy has been a centre of population for a very long time. Some remains from the Neolithic Age (8000 b.c.) have been found. In later times the place became a Roman settlement with a hill fort overlooking the lowlands. Sandy used to have two railway stations almost side by side. The 'east' station met its demise in the Beeching era and was on a cross country route from Cambridge to Bedford, a distance of some twenty-five miles. Today to travel by train between these two county towns would involve going via London . . . well over 100 miles!

Leaving Sandy station on the 'down' (west) side follow the approach road and then turn to the right over the bridge. Thereafter turn left along a secondary road, signposted to Everton. This road soon rises amongst pleasantly wooded areas. After a short half mile and at an intersection of roads go straight on through a gate following a track which soon descends to a further gate, with the wooded ground bending away to your right. You are now on . . .

THE GREENSAND WAY which has wended its way across flatter country since its path through a larger section of the Greensand Hills in the neighbourhood of Leighton Buzzard. These hills consisting of a bright sandy soil circumnavigate the London Basin, offshoots occuring in Kent, Surrey and Hampshire, etc. Where you are now the Greensand Way is also a site of a Roman road leading in a northerly direction from the hill fort at Sandy.

Passing through yet another gate, you pass a spinney like belt of trees on your right, known as the Hassell Hedge (obviously a corruption of the word, Hazzell), the grounds on your right being the parkland surrounding a mansion called Hazzells Hall. After crossing a concreted driveway the way continues straight ahead. The track you are on soon itself acquires a concrete surface and passes some farm buildings and a small water tank on your left. Here turn sharp right on a signposted footpath with the hedge on your left. At the end of the field cross a stile, shortly followed by another and continue forward rising quite steeply uphill. To your left opens out a great view of . . .

THE IVEL AND OUSE BASINS . . . a vast expanse of flattish land that stretches in the west to North Buckinghamshire and in the north to (what was) Huntingdonshire . . . now absorbed by Cambridgeshire. If visibility is reasonable you will see in the middle distance GRAFHAM WATER one of the largest artificial lakes in southern England, its surface covering an area of over three square miles.

At the top of the rise cross a further stile and follow a little green track which soon leads out into a road. Here turn left and after about a quarter of a mile you are in the centre of . . .

EVERTON a quiet and somewhat spread out village perched on the higher ground. The village church which lies just beyond the main crossroads used to be in a detached portion of the county of Huntingdonshire and of the parish of Tetworth. Of the latter there is no trace nowadays, the church and surrounding village are lost without trace.

At the village centre is the impressive . . .

THORNTON ARMS which amongst other things sells excellent local beers from the County of Bedford and a wide and very reasonably priced selection of bar meals. From a conversation with the licensee one gathers that the establishment is frequently used by ramblers and that this pleasant inn has featured in at least one other 'pub walk' book.

Leaving the Thornton Arms retrace your steps along the secondary road from which you emerged and follow this for about three-quarters of a mile to a point where wooded ground commences on your left. Enter the wooded area by a rough drive. In some quarter of a mile you come to a junction of tracks where you turn to the right. This track continues in a straight line for a mile across . . .

SANDY HEATH which has been reclaimed from its original state and now devoted to agriculture and forestry. Small patches of gorse or broom are evident indicating the original nature of the terrain.

At a T-junction of tracks go left soon joining a 'B' road where you turn right shortly descending amongst trees to join the outward route and over the railway bridge and leftwards into the station yard.

Walk 2

BIGGLEWADE to 'the March Hare', DUNTON, and back

BY RAIL . . . West Anglia Great Northern Trains (Great Northern Electrics) from London (Kings Cross) via Hatfield, Stevenage and Hitchin.

BY ROAD . . . via A1(M) to turn off for Biggleswade town along A6001.

MAP . . . Ordnance Survey Landranger Sheet 153.

DISTANCE OF WALK . . . Approximately 6 miles.

TOPOGRAPHY . . . This is a ramble that traverses wide open spaces with nothing but the tiniest of undulations. The tract of country involved is part of the great plain that extends from the Fenlands across to Cambridgeshire and into Eastern Bedfordshire. It is unlikely that you will see any cattle or sheep for this is agricultural country, truly part of 'the Granary of England'. The walk is equally suitable for a warm summer day or a dry day in winter when the east wind is howling amongst the hedgerows. The going underfoot can be distinctly 'tacky', particularly across the middle of fields. Congratulations to the local authority for so clearly waymarking the rights of way. In the absence of these some of the little used paths could be difficult to follow. A unique feature of this ramble is that no stiles have to be negotiated!

BIGGLESWADE is a medium-sized town on the route of the Great North Road and of the main railway line from London to Edinburgh. Before the coming of the railway the River Ivel which runs just west of the town was navigable. It is a traditional type of English town

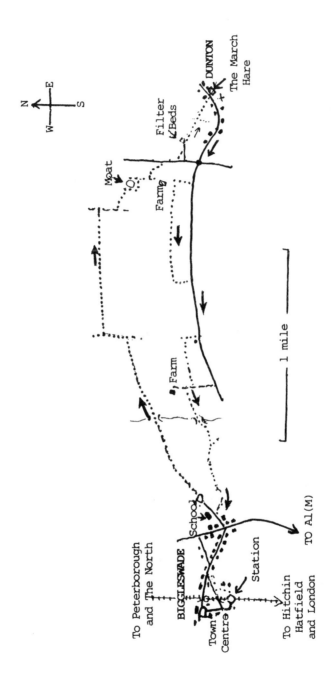

with a large rectangular market place, nowadays surrounded by the 'multiples', inns, Building Society branches, cafés, etc. As is the case with other towns on the A1 road, Biggleswade is now 'by-passed'. Inevitably there has been development around the fringes of the town . . . commuters to the City can travel by rail to London in little over half an hour. The now privatised railway has given a new name to the region. They style it as 'West Anglia', i.e. it is on the western side of what we all know as East Anglia! The town is now the centre of an extensive agricultural area.

Leaving Biggleswade via the 'up' (east) side turn left after crossing the footbridge and follow an alley which soon leads out into a quiet road, aptly named Back Street. Those wishing to visit the town centre before the walk should turn left here, otherwise go to the right. You soon join a main road which follows ahead, shortly passing the local municipal offices on your left. Approaching a major junction of roads cross (with care) to the opposite pavement. At the junction cross the road leading to Potton (B1040) to a side road with 'no through road' signs. This byeway passes a school on you left and ends at a turning circle for motor traffic. The route lies ahead to the left of the circle and becomes a farm track. Hereabouts after a matter of 15 minutes walking you are in totally rural surroundings. If you look ahead and slightly to the right you will see, if visibility permits, the tower of Dunton church which is close to your destination.

The track descends very slightly and crosses a ditch via a concrete bridge. The route lies straight on across a junction of paths and eventually at a point where pylon wires cross above, you come to a crossing track. Here go left some some 50 yards and then turn right with a hedge and a substantial drainage ditch on your right. Where the hedge veers off to the right continue on over an open field aiming for a waymark which is just to the right of an isolated tree. Here cross a 'surfaced' farm road and over a further field. The direction followed is very slightly rightwards to another waymark which is to the right of some isolated bushes. Here you join another track where you turn right. Follow this track for a couple of hundred yards or so to a point where a waymark guides you sharp leftwards towards some wooded ground. On approaching the trees it will be seen that just inside the area is a deep ditch. This is the remains of the moat surrounding . . .

NEWTONBURY. The suffix bury around here indicates that it was a large dwelling house and this stood on the outskirts of the hamlet of Newton which consists nowadays of a large farm only. Of Newtonbury itself there is no trace, it having fallen into disuse many years ago. In the thicket of overgrowth, the only sign of habitation nowadays is a forlorn row of apparently disused beehives. The author was told that the locality within the moat is sometimes devoted to clay pigeon shoots.

On reaching the moat turn right and then left, with the moat on your left. You then join a farm road which follow to the right for some 100 yards to a point where a waymark indicates that the right of way directs you to turn left. After some 30 yards another helpful waymark indicates that you take a half-right direction to the left-hand corner of the field where you join a secondary road. Going forward on this road you soon reach footpath signs. Here turn left crossing the corner of a field joining after only a few yards a concreted driveway, which follow to the gates leading into some filter beds. To the right of the gates follow the footpath which now becomes enclosed. Keep in a forward direction with the tower of the church ahead and ignoring a cross path you emerge by the side of a house in the centre of ...

DUNTON, a rather spread out village isolated in a vast area of agricultural land. New buildings outnumber the old but peace and quiet prevail, the locality being away from main routes or 'classified' roads.

Across the road and with the background of the fine old village church is ...

THE MARCH HARE, a capacious country inn serving the community of Dunton and its surroundings. In this ultra-friendly local, bar snacks are usually available at midday. A lesser selection of snacks are willingly supplied at other times. A request to the licencee or his wife will elicit what is currently available. Two cask beers were on offer, Wadsworths 6X from far away Devizes in Wiltshire and surprise, surprise, MILD ale from Boddingtons of Manchester. One finds that mild ale from the cask is very rarely available south of the Midlands.

Leaving the March Hare go left along the village street. After a half mile you arrive at a crossroads. Here keep forward. The next turning on the right is a farm road. Follow this road (notices proclaim that the road is private but it is a right of way for walkers).

Where the road enters the farm turn sharp left along a footpath, which follow for a good half mile where a ditch and hedge confront you. Here turn left with the hedge and ditch on your right to emerge again into the road. Turn right here and some quarter of a mile ahead just before passing a house on your right, turn right along a track which follows on your left a belt of trees and shrubs. You soon encounter a waymark indicating a crossing place of paths. Here go left through the belt of shrubland and thence over an open field to arrive at a 'surfaced' farm road. Here go right for a few yards to cross a ditch and then sharp left with the ditch on your left. At the end of the field a new and substantial footbridge crosses a stream.

Having crossed the bridge go left across a ditch by means of a plank bridge and immediately turn right with the ditch now on your right. You soon join a rough track. Here turn right and follow the track which winds round to eventually join the outward route just short of the road junction. Thence follow the main road into the town, veering leftwards when you come to Back Street, thence left along the alley to the station.

Walk 3

HARLINGTON to 'the Lynford Arms', SHARPENHOE, and back

BY RAIL . . . Harlington Station is on the Midland Main Line from London to Bedford. Stopping trains are provided by 'Thameslink' services at ½ hourly intervals from Brighton, Croydon, London Bridge, and Kings Cross (Thameslink), etc., calling at St. Albans and Luton *en route*.

BY ROAD . . . from north or south, M1 junction 12, thence northwards on A5120 (as for Bedford). In just over a ¼ mile, turn right along an unclassified road signposted to Harlington. The station and car park are on your right as you approach the village.

MAP . . . Ordnance Survey Landranger sheet 166.

DISTANCE OF WALK . . . Approximately 5 miles.

TOPOGRAPHY . . . In the main this ramble peregrinates around the undulating pastures of South Bedfordshire, the footpaths in this region being nowadays well signposted and waymarked. As an exception the portion of the route some two miles from the beginning involves a really steep (but short) climb of the Chiltern escarpment to the hills south of Sharpenhoe village. The summit level, known as Sharpenhoe Clappers, offers a vast belvedere across the South Midlands with a coombe on its west wide in every way as dramatic as the better known Devil's Punch Bowl in Surrey. More adventure is to follow. The way from the hilltop to the pub consists of 159 steep and uneven stairs. Descent of this veritable Jacobs Ladder should be made with extreme care (the text of the ramble gives an alternative route which should be followed by those who are not so sure footed). The tiny hamlet of Sharpenhoe (within the parish of neighbouring Streatley) is a quiet place to halt for refreshment, and the ensuing 2 miles back to Harlington are in the main fairly flat offering a relaxing end to the day.

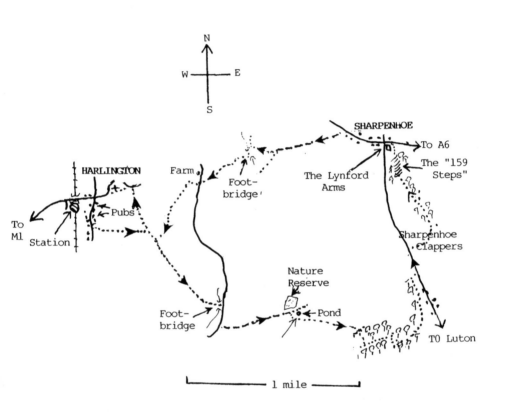

N

W — E

S

SHARPENHOE

To A6

The "159 Steps"

HARLINGTON

Farm

Foot-bridge

The Lynford Arms

Pubs

To Ml

Station

Sharpenhoe Clappers

Nature Reserve

Foot-bridge

Pond

TO Luton

└──────── 1 mile ────────┘

HARLINGTON, set upon a hillock amid the lowlands of South Bedfordshire, typifies all that is traditional of an English village. It has two cosy pubs, a lovely old parish church, a village hall, a village green with cricket matches in the season, and a war memorial shrouded in trees at the main crossroads.

Leaving Harlington Station by the approach road, turn right and cross the line. The road rises for some 150 yards. By the war memorial, turn right passing 'the Carpenters Arms' and a little further on 'the Old Sun'. A short way ahead, opposite house number 62 turn left along an enclosed path which soon emerges into a field. The way lies ahead slightly diagonally to the right. Having traversed this field you come to a T-junction of footpaths by a waymark. Here turn right descending gradually to a further junction of ways. At this point the route lies ahead, access to which is through the bushes on your right. The path soon crosses a ditch by a plank bridge and continues across the middle of a very large field. You eventually come to the remainder of an old hedgerow. Here veer left soon crossing a plank bridge. The stream below is a 'feeder' to the tiny . . .

RIVER FLIT which rises in the hills some 2 miles to the north. Going north from the London Basin this is the first stream that eventually empties its water into The Wash between the counties of Lincolnshire and Norfolk. Although the source of another river, the Lee (or Lea) is only a mile or so away from that of the Flit, the waters of the Lea disport themselves into the Thames via London's Docklands and thereafter into the estuary between North Kent and South Essex. The ground between these two river sources is known geographically as a watershed.

Having crossed the bridge you immediately emerge into a tiny road. This quiet 'highway' literally leads from nowhere to nowhere serving just one farm during its course. Consequently it is practically free from traffic! You turn right in this byway and after a quarter of a mile, you leave it by means of a signposted bridlepath to your left. Follow this gravelly way for a short ½ mile to a point where there is a fenced nature reserve. Here, just before reaching a quiet pond on the right, turn right into a large field. On entering the field a waymark points the direction of the path, something less than diagonal. Aim for a point in the wooded hills ahead at a place where there is a raised area between two 'dips', and enter the woods by a makeshift stile consisting of a couple of sawn-off tree trunks and the intervening wire fencing. Cross the path that runs just inside the fencing and go half right along a little pathway that ascends steeply through the wooded ground.

About three-quarters of the way up the hill, there is on your left a bench seat which provides a welcome place to rest with far-flung views of South Bedfordshire and beyond ahead. A short way beyond the seat there is a T-junction of paths. Here turn left and follow the undulating path which in a matter of 100 yards or so leads to a well waymarked meeting place of tracks. Here go ahead as directed by the Icknield Way sign. (For information on this ancient highway, see page 66.) You are just inside the border of the woods on your right hand side, and above the steeply descending ground on your left. About a quarter mile on the track veers right outside the woods and then left with the trees on your immediate left. Soon the track makes a right hand turn away from the woods and in a few yards you emerge into a road where you turn left. At a car park a little way on leave the public road by turning right through posts to a private service road which is reserved for national Trust vehicles only. As the informative notice board tells you, this area is known as . . .

SHARPENHOE CLAPPERS, the name deriving from the French word 'clapiers' meaning rabbit holes! This lovely local beauty spot with its woods, hills, and views was once the site of a prehistoric hill fort.

Follow the tarred service road to a left-hand corner where it becomes a track. Where the track turns sharply to the right, go leftwards descending now between trees and bushes. At a fork in the path ahead take the left-hand alternative and proceed ahead with a wire fence on your left overlooking a virtual precipice, on the side of which a herd of black sheep may be grazing. Soon the path meets another from the right. Continuing ahead you are confronted by a steep flight of 159 steps. The steps are largely uneven and care should be exercised on the descent. *For the not so sure footed or those having symptoms of vertigo the descent can be made by way of the public road which descends beyond the car park.* At the foot of the steps the path follows the left-hand side of a small field and soon descends into a road. Here turn left and you are in the hamlet of . . .

SHARPENHOE, a sleepy place, without shop or church, nestling at the foot of the great Chiltern escarpment. Only a mile or so away to the east is the A6 trunk road from London to the North, which at this point by-passes the substantial village of Barton-le-Clay, until comparatively recent times known as Barton in the Clay. As the Chilterns give way to the pastures of South Beds., the subsoil changes from mainly chalk to clay.

On the left is . . .

THE LYNFORD ARMS, situated at the junction of by-roads, with a little north-facing green at its front complete with 'beer tables' for alfresco refreshment. The Lynford Arms is a cosy place inside with two bars and with cask ales from the North, the Midlands, and the South. The bar food menu contains many alternatives and is exceptionally competitively priced.

Leave the pub via the road signposted back to Harlington 2¼ miles (it is only 2 miles via the route of this ramble). Where the houses of the village end and after crossing a small stream fork left along a signposted path that rises gradually on the right-hand side of a large field. You encounter a parting of ways after about a half of a mile, and here take the right-hand fork which descends a little passing through a small clump of trees, and then follows the line of

29

a small ditch. Where this path veers to the right go sharp left over a stream.

Having crossed the water via a substantial footbridge with railings, the clear path veers to the left and then to the right and a forward course soon picks up the line of a hedge on your right. Winding along by this hedge you emerge shortly into the tiny road that was encountered on the outward route. Cross the road to a path opposite which goes in a half-right direction with a deep ditch on your right. After some 30 yards the path veers half left with the ditch now on the left. Continue ahead and you shortly arrive at the junction of paths where you meet your steps of the outwards journey. Turn right retracing your steps, but at the waymark, where you emerged from the field earlier, go straight on along rising ground, soon passing a wooded area on your left. On emerging into the road go left and almost immediately where the road bends to the right go ahead along a tarred path across a recreation ground to rejoin the road to the left of the church and so ahead and downhill by the crossroads and war memorial to the bridge by the station.

Walk 4

FLITWICK to 'The Star and Garter', SILSOE and back

BY RAIL . . . Thameslink trains from Brighton, Croydon, London, Luton, etc. from the south. From Bedford in the north. Service interval at least ½ hourly.

BY ROAD . . . Leave M1 and Junction 12, thence A5120 to Flitwick. A5120 also provides access to Dunstable in a southerly direction, and from the north from Bedford via A418.

MAP . . . Ordnance Survey Landranger Sheet 153.

DISTANCE OF WALK . . . Approximately 7½ miles.

TOPOGRAPHY . . . The area covered is mainly amid the flat country which forms the basin of the river Flit, see page 27. Towards the end of the outgoing route there is a rise of some 50 feet and a similar ridge is encountered at the start of the return journey. For those who have an aversion to hill climbing, it is a classic. The paths are in reasonable condition all the year round although the clay in this region can become 'tacky' after a wet spell. Once out of the built up area of Flitwick, the country is extremely peaceful, the three villages encountered *en route* being both tiny and remote from present day 'improvements'. The most interesting feature passed both on the inward and outward routes is the wild and wooded expanse known as Flitwick Moor. This is not a moor such as you would find in say, Devon or Yorkshire, but is a completely flat tract of land, criss-crossed with dykes, streams, and drainage ditches. The moor consists of a peat bog that has been allowed to revert to its natural state. Such examples are rare and Flitwick Moor is the last remaining terrain of its kind in the county.

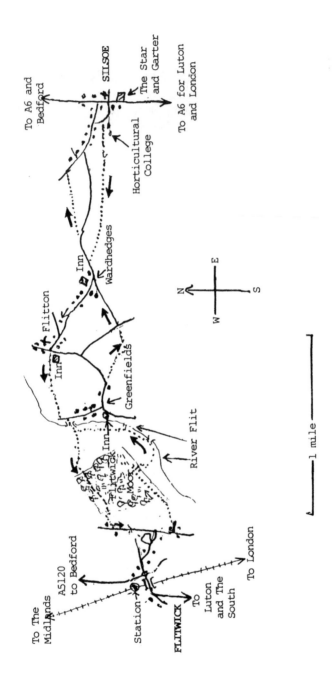

To A6 and
Bedford

SILSOE

The Star
and Garter

To A6 for Luton
and London

Horticultural
College

Wardhedges

Inn

Flitton

Inn

Greenfields

River Flit

N   E
W   S

FLITWICK Inn

Flitwick
Moor

A5120
to Bedford

To The
Midlands

Station

FLITWICK

To
Luton
and The
South

To London

1 mile

FLITWICK has grown so much in recent years that it has become something of a 'suburb of nowhere'. The old village lies some ½ mile to the south-west of the railway station, the area around the latter being a labyrinth of residential thoroughfares. The hub of all this development is the bridge across the railway, by the station. It is, let us say, not an attractive place as far as scenery goes, but it surely gives solace to those who return to Bedfordshire after a stressful day in the City of London! So much for that . . . the locality is set amongst peaceful agricultural country and a matter of 10 minutes' walk leaves the built-up area behind you.

Leaving the station cross the bridge and go straight across the busy road into a quieter road, The Avenue. Shortly go to the right along Easton Road. Ignoring a crescent on your left keep to the right and you soon emerge into a mainish sort of thoroughfare. Here turn right. After some 100 yards take the turning on your left, Moor Lane. Just before reaching the end of this short road look for a clear path on your left and follow the ensuing track which soon enters wooded ground. You are now at . . .

FLITWICK MOOR, a nature reserve that is reputed to be the last peat bog left in the County of Bedfordshire. Rare birds and even rarer plant species are found within the limits of this marshy and wooded area.

Entering the woods the most used path beers off to the left. Ignore this and follow a minor path ahead which is accompanied by a ditch on your right. Apart from 'wiggling' round trees this little path keeps its forward course and soon leads out into a gravelly track, where you turn right over a bridge and then out of the woods through a gate which leads into some open ground keeping to the right of this ground to its far corner. Here go right for a pace or two, and then left and over a footbridge where you turn right following the margin of a large field.

Follow the edge of the field round and you soon find that on your right is the swift flowing river Flit. Ignoring a 'vehicle size' bridge on your right and a little further on a slender footbridge, the path enters some bushy ground soon leaving it and emerging into a meadow. Go straight on here (ignore the path which forks to the left) and at the end of the meadow veer right over a footbridge with railings and on for a few yards through a green way and into a minor road where go right. You are entering the hamlet of . . .

GREENFIELDS, a remote place consisting of a 'dead end' lane leading out into a secondary road. On the latter there is a village pub and on the former a Methodist chapel.

The minor road in which you emerge is the aforementioned dead end. Follow this past the Methodist chapel and some attractive cottages out into a secondary road where you turn left. In a short ¼ mile the road takes a sweep to the left. Here cross and follow a clearly defined footpath which goes across diagonally to a wire fence and then bends right for a few yards to the corner of the fence. Here turn sharp left and immediately sharp right across a somewhat decrepit 'one plank' footbridge over a ditch. Having negotiated the bridge go sharp left again and follow the clear path which leads out into a T-junction of fairly minor roads. Cross to the road opposite (signposted to Silsoe) and continue for a half mile on to an intersection of roads at the hamlet of . . .

WARDHEDGES, which consists of just a few houses and a pub, the Coopers Arms. The ground here is a little higher than the surrounding plains.

Passing the road junction with the pub just around the corner on the right the road rises a little, then bends to the right. Here keep straight ahead along a bridleway that descends to join another road, where turn to the right. Follow this road for a good ½ mile, ignoring turnings to the right and left you arrive in the High Street of . . .

SILSOE, a pleasant village on what used to be the A6 trunk road from London to the North. Happily to say there is now a by-pass road so comparative quiet reigns. There is an old adage which says that you cannot have things both ways. When the by-pass was built it went through the grounds of neighbouring Wrest Park thus bisecting the peaceful driveway from the village to the mansion. Wrest Park is now the home of an agricultural college.

On entering the High Street, turn right. After passing the church on your left you arrive at . . .

THE STAR AND GARTER, a fine old inn with a considerable capacity inside for its patrons. Four cask ales including Flowers I.P.A. are served, the latter with its ABV (Alcohol by Volume) in the region of 3.5 being an excellent mid-day tipple when there is walking still to be done. There is an extensive menu of competitively priced bar snacks augmented by more substantial meals, details of which are displayed on a blackboard.

Leaving the pub retrace your steps for a few yards and take the turning to the left opposite the church. The road soon bends round to the right and as it does you veer to the left following a track which passes through the grounds of a horticultural college. Follow the track on over a low ridge. After some three-quarters of a mile you emerge into a road. Here you follow the route of the outgoing journey for a few yards, then taking the right hand fork past the Coopers Arms. The road descends out of the village of Wardhedges and in some half mile emerges at a T-junction with a church on the right at the village of . . .

FLITTON, another settlement with little but a series of attractive cottages, a large parish church, and the White Hart pub. In the distant past Silsoe was in the parish of Flitton and the nobility from Wrest Park were buried here. Thus explains the reason why the road from Silsoe to Flitton is not only hedged but tree-lined . . . a dignified route for the cortege.

At the junction of roads the route lies straight ahead on to a footpath that enters the gate of house number 3. For a few paces you are in the private garden of the hourse, after which the path becomes enclosed and soon emerges into a field. Follow the right hand side of the field and shortly before the gap into the next field turn sharp right across a footbridge over a ditch and then sharp left following the hedge at the left hand side of the field. At the next field the path goes through the middle and emerges into the end of a lane. Follow this for some 20 yards and turn right. You will have recognised the spot as the dead end lane from Greenfields village. Cross the river Flit by the bridge with railings. On the outward route you emerged from the path on your left. Ignore this now and continue diagonally across the field to its far corner. At the next field veer to the right and enter again the wooded ground of Flitwick Moor.

Follow the main path ahead. On your left is an area of swamp with reeds growing in brackish water. You soon cross a bridge under which flows the water from a nearby . . .

CHALYBEATE SPRING. On account of the iron content of this stream the water is a golden yellow colour. The medicinal properties of these waters are famed and constitute the beverages available at some famous spas.

Keep a forward direction over the 'iron water' bridge and soon leave the woods and emerge into a track, where turn right. In a few yards the track makes a left-hand turn. (Note at this point an interesting geological map and legend relating to the moor in a frame on your right.) The track soon leads out into a busy road. Here turn left. In ¼ mile you come to the turning on the right from which you emerged at the beginning of the ramble. Retrace your steps along Easton Road and The Avenue back to Flitwick Station.

Walk 5

LINSLADE (Leighton Buzzard Station) to 'the Dove Inn', WING, and back

BY RAIL ... On main (North London Railways) line from London (Euston) via Watford, Hemel Hempstead, etc. From the north via Milton Keynes to Leighton Buzzard. Three trains per hour on weekdays, one an hour on Sundays (possibly two in summer).

BY ROAD ... A41 from London area, thence A418 from Aylesbury. Junction 20 of M25 connects with A41. Alternatively leave M1 at Junction 13 thence A418 to Leighton Buzzard, through town centre to Linslade in which the station is situated.

MAP ... Ordnance Survey Landranger Sheet 165.

DISTANCE OF WALK ... Approximately 5 miles.

TOPOGRAPHY ... From the valley of the river Ouzel, you rise some 300 feet to the exposed village of Wing which overlooks the vast Vale of Aylesbury, with the Chiltern Hills as a backdrop. The outward route is remote and very rural, contrasting with the return journey which because of a 'cancelled footpath' follows for some way on the verge of the A418 road, from which there are great views across the valley to the pine woods of the Greensand Ridge in the neighbourhood of Heath and Reach and the Brickhills. The clay hereabouts can hold water for a long time, so be prepared for soggy conditions after rain. The footpaths followed on the route outwards to Wing appear, somewhat surprisingly, to be little used and a note should be made that at some field boundaries there are no stiles or gates and at one point nearing Waterloo Farm what can only be described as an 'obstacle' has to be crossed. This is something of a cross breed between a stile and a fence and good balance is essential to surmount it! The author has written to the local authorities requesting more orthodox access to these delightful footpaths and it is hoped that after publication of this book some remedial action will have been taken.

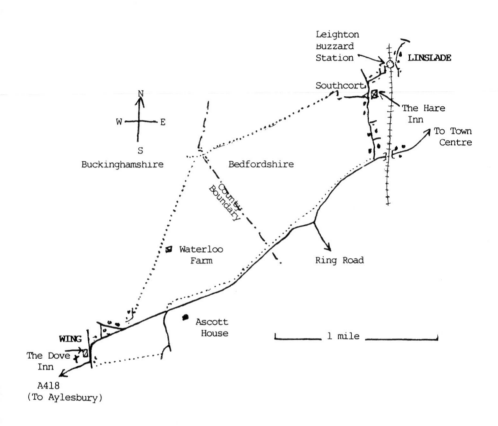

Leighton Buzzard Station

LINSLADE

Southcort

The Hare Inn

To Town Centre

N
W — E
S

Buckinghamshire

Bedfordshire

County Boundary

Waterloo Farm

Ring Road

WING

Ascott House

1 mile

The Dove Inn

A418
(To Aylesbury)

A WORD to those who are not as agile as they used to be. This walk on the outward journey encounters a delightfully rural path, which currently suffers from the fact that stiles are conspicuous by their absence. This involves climbing over or crawling under at least two '2-bar' fences, and later on negotiating a highish stile without crossbars for the feet. The author has written to the local authorities involved and the replies from each promise hope that the defects will soon be remedied, making the paths in question more 'user friendly'.

LINSLADE where the ramble begins contains within its purlieus Leighton Buzzard station. This small town grew up around what was then the London and North Western Railway. Linslade is separated from Leighton Buzzard by the tiny river Ouzel. At one time the river was the county boundary between Bedfordshire and Buckingham-shire, but boundary changes earlier this century have encompassed both parishes within the former.

Leave the station on the 'down' side, i.e. the side away from the main station buildings. On emerging from the footbridge turn left into a residential road which soon veers round to the right. On joining another road continue in the same direction eventually arriving at a small green with the Hare Inn on your left. Opposite the inn cross the green and follow a small lane which shortly peters out to become a track. The track takes a turn to the right and then to the left and ends at a gate. The path becomes enclosed between a fence and hedge on the right hand side of the field. (Should the enclosed path be obstructed by bushes, you should cross the fence and proceed along the outside.) At the end of the field cross a two-bar fence*. The path continues in a forward direction just to the left-hand side of the 'valley bottom' and continues to ascend to another two bar fence* at the far left-hand corner of the field. Crossing this fence the path continues along the left-hand margin of the next field.

The path soon arrives at a well waymarked junction of routes. Here you should take a few paces to the right and then go left into a small thicket. After a few paces, leave the thicket and turn left along a path which runs diagonally across a largish field passing an electricity pylon on your left. The way into the next field is via the

---

* *Conventinal stiles may be provided by the time of publication.*

'obstacle stile', i.e. lacking in crossbars for the feet. The path then descends slightly to pass to the right-hand side of Waterloo Farm, passing three (this time conventional) stiles in quick succession. After the third stile the path follows a course a little way from the right-hand hedge and then veering back to the hedge to cross another stile next to a gate. From here the way lies diagonally across the next field emerging via a swing gate into a small road with houses opposite. Turn left here soon arriving at the main road access to which is across a strip of greensward. Follow this main road for about ½ mile to the centre of the village of . . .

WING, a breezy hilltop place overlooking the great Vale of Aylesbury. One of the features of the Vale is that many of the villages thereon are perched upon isolated uplands; indeed some way to the east of here is the village of Quainton from which it is reputed that if visibility permits you can see the hills of Wales! Although Wing stands upon the main highway from Leighton Buzzard to Aylesbury it is a pleasant enough place in which to bide.

After the road takes a bend left you see a few yards ahead . . .

THE DOVE INN, fronting directly on to the road, this is a cosy place within. There is cask beer, and a limited but competitive menu of snacks and sandwiches. The place exudes an air of friendliness. It is significant that the author asked for a popular 'snack' which was not listed on the menu, but which was gladly produced on request. So very different from a pub managed by a 'chain' in the Surrey commuter belt where the same dish was selected (it was on a menu). The author here was curtly told by a young barmaid that he was looking at the children's menu, and accordingly he was too old! In short, full marks to the Dove for the cordial welcome and for the service received.

Leaving the Dove follow the main road for a few yards and where it bends off to the right, keep forward along an unclassified road, with great views of the Vale ahead. The escarpment of the Chilterns forms the backdrop. Looking slightly to your left you will see in the distance the lion carved in the chalk in the vicinity of Whipsnade Wild Animal Park. After you have passed the last dwelling house on your left, turn left and follow a clear path which dips down to cross a small brook and thereafter keeps forward to join a lane just to the right of a house. Follow the lane which climbs uphill and ignore a turning to the right signposted to Ledburn. You shortly pass the drive of . . .

ASCOTT HOUSE which is owned by the National Trust, and which is open to the public during the summer months. Unfortunately there is no right of way through the grounds.

Arriving at a T-junction with the main A418 road, cross this with care to the far side and turn to the right. It is fortunate that this side of the road has a sizeable verge and a footpath for pedestrians for it is imperative from here that this highway be followed for some 1½ miles. (There *was* a footpath that ran somewhat parallel on the right for some way, but this seems to have disappeared in the name of 'progress', its course having been dissected by the new Leighton Buzzard ring road!) The roadside path has come compensations. At one point the A418 has been diverted slightly and for a quiet stretch you are accompanied by nothing but the ghost of the old highway. Then looking ahead and to a lefward direction are great views across the Ouzel valley, where the river is accompanied by the Grand Union Canal, the main railway and a link road between Linslade and the A5. Beyond the valley you will see the pine woods of the Greensand Hills around 'the Brickhill' villages, (Great Brickhill, Little Brickhill and Bow Brickhill).

You descend to a point where there is a railway bridge ahead. Before the bridge turn left along Bunkers Lane which soon leads to the Hare Inn, after passing which veer right and follow the outgoing route back to the station.

Walk 6

WATFORD (Met. Station) to 'the Clarendon Arms', CHANDLERS CROSS and back

BY RAIL . . . London Underground (Metropolitan Line) from Baker Street. If using main Euston–Northampton line, alight at Watford Junction station. Cross town via Station Road, St. Albans Road and Rickmansworth Road – about 1¼ miles. Some bus services available on weekdays or Saturdays. Watford West Station is not recommended as there is currently only one train a day – in the early morning!

BY ROAD . . . Station Approach is a turning off Rickmansworth Road and three-quarters of a mile west of Watford Town Centre. The town is accessible from the M1 via junctions 5 or 6. Alternative route from London is via A40 (Western Avenue) turning off at Northolt on to A4180 through Ruislip to join A404 towards Rickmansworth, then right via A4145. From North West direction A41 from Hemel Hempstead and Aylesbury, etc.

MAPS . . . Ordnance Survey Pathfinder Sheets 166 or 176.

DISTANCE OF WALK . . . Approximately 5¼ miles.

TOPOGRAPHY . . . A nice quiet piece of country at the very edge of the Chiltern Hills. This well-wooded landscape lies just within the orbit of the M25 motorway. The municipal district is known as Three Rivers on account of the confluence of the Rivers Gade, Colne and Chess. The paths are all clear and well used. An ideal ramble for a 'first go' at country walking. The only strenuous stretch is a short and steep rise through a belt of trees on the return journey.

WATFORD (Underground Station) to The Clarendon Arms, Chandlers Cross

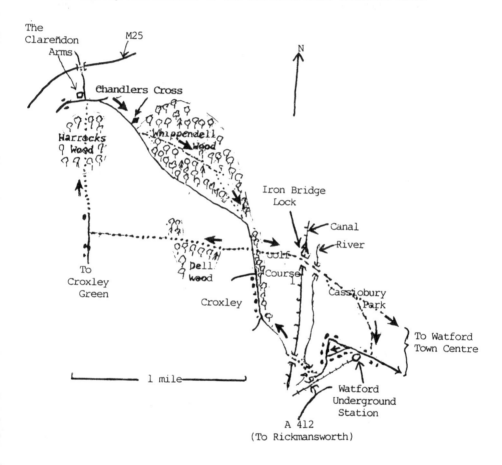

WATFORD can be described as a provincial town just outside the Metropolitan areas of London. It is not however an unpleasant place, notwithstanding the fact that it has in recent years acquired the accoutrements of a shopping mall, a pedestrianised High Street, and 'ring roads', etc. It abounds with pubs, cafes, and restaurants and used to be the home of a famous brewing company, Benskins. Their 'light mild' cask ale was a favourite beverage throughout the Chiltern area, and their rich dark bottled 'Colne Springs' was amongst the strongest brews of Southern England. It is said by some that after you have passed through Watford you are in the North of England – not of course true, but none the less the town is a 'buffer state' between the suburbs of London and the countryside that lies beyond.

The ramble begins at Watford Underground Station which is in a quiet residential area on the extreme western edge of the town. Turn left on leaving the station and after a matter of some 75 yards, fork left into Swiss Avenue which descends to join Gade Avenue. After a right hand turn and in the greensward on the right will be seen a wooden footbridge over the River Gade. Cross this bridge and follow the clear path that soon joins a small road which shortly crosses the Grand Union Canal by a hump-backed bridge. The ensuing narrow lane rises and falls to widen out and continue with houses and bungalows on the left and a steep bank of woodland on the right. You are here at the extremities of ...

CROXLEY which with neighbouring Croxley Green forms a quiet backwater of suburban development which grew in the early part of the century when the Metropolitan Railway came. Croxley Mills are famous for their paper. The green itself lies some one mile to the east, and contains pleasant pubs.

Having passed the dwellings go ahead on a lane signposted as a 'no through road'. In a matter of just over ¼ mile turn left at a public footpath sign. The path ascends gently over the middle of a field and soon joins wooded ground on your left. Keep ahead by the wooded area, eventually coming to a junction of paths. Once again the route runs forward, the path now becoming enclosed, emerging in just over ½ mile into a tiny tarred lane. Here turn right. Having passed a house on your left, the lane peters out and becomes a grassy track, which soon leads into Harrocks Wood. The route lies straight ahead through this delightful woodland, emerging into a tiny enclosed path which in a few yards leads out into a road at ...

CHANDLERS CROSS, a quiet locality of homesteads, set around junctions of minor roads. Its peace is only disturbed by the muffled roar of traffic on the M25 motorway which pursues its course some few hundreds of yards to the north.

On emerging from the footpath, across the road is . . .

THE CLARENDON ARMS, a lovely country inn at the intersection of two roads. There is ample accommodation for refreshment both inside and outside. Meals are served every day, and the 'regular' cask ales are Marston's bitter and 'Pedigree', a stronger version from the same brewer. Fuller's 'London Pride' makes up the trio, which is augmented by a guest beer.

On leaving the inn, go forward as signposted to Watford and in a few yards take a fork on the right into a narrow lane, marked 'no through road' which follows, passing nurseries on your left, after which turn left into woods. At a junction a few yards ahead, take the right hand fork, and then a few paces further on ignore a further path which forks right. The path that you are following has a 'no horse riding' sign. After passing two small clearings on the right, take the main of two paths. When the main path is descending you come to a further intersection of woodland ways, just by a lone coniferous tree on your immediate left. Here fork to the right and gently downhill soon passing a notice indicating that you are on a nature trail. You will soon emerge at a narrow lane, where go left. (Should you by chance take a wrong turning in the woods keep on to the perimeter of the wooded ground and go right to join the specified route.)

In some 100 yards or so you reach a place where a public footpath crosses the lane. (You may recognise this as the place where you turned left on the outward route.) Now, to avoid duplicating the route go left and follow a clear path which steeply ascends a well-wooded bank. You emerge amidst the greens and fairways of the West Herts Golf Club, the path continuing straight ahead. As the notices warn, take care of balls being driven across your course. Then the footpath descends through a bushy area, crosses a way used by the golfers, and descends further to cross the canal close to ...

IRON BRIDGE LOCK, one of the many locks by which the canal ascends to cross over the watershed near Tring. The canal originates in West London and links the capital with Birmingham and the West Midlands.

The path then crosses a river and becomes tarred at the entry to ...

CASSIOBURY PARK, which since its mansion was demolished in 1922 has become a public park whose main gates abut almost at the centre of Watford Town.

Follow the main path straight ahead rising slightly and in a short ½ mile go right to emerge at park gates adjacent to a tea house and toilets, and emerging into a road turn right for the station.

Walk 7

KINGS LANGLEY to 'the Cart and Horses', COMMONWOOD and back

BY RAIL . . . Kings Langley Station is on the direct line from London (Euston) to Northampton via Harrow and Watford. Coming south from Northampton the route is via Milton Keynes, Leighton Buzzard, and Tring, etc. A half-hourly service operates on weekdays; hourly on Sundays.

BY ROAD . . . From London area, A41 to intersection with M25 north of Watford. Thence follow A4251 for ½ mile, taking first right and first right again to Kings Langley Station. From a northerly direction, follow M1 to Junction 8, and on to Hemel Hempstead town picking up A4251 in a southerly direction. After passing through Kings Langley village, turn left in some three-quarters of a mile and then right into station.

MAPS . . . Ordnance Survey Landranger Sheet 166, or Ordnance Survey Pathfinder Sheets 1139 and 1120.

DISTANCE OF WALK . . . Approximately 5½ miles.

TOPOGRAPHY . . . The gentle slopes west of the valley of the River Gade lead to a remote corner of Hertfordshire. It is difficult to imagine that only some five miles away are the hubbub of Watford's shopping centre or the satellite town of Hemel Hempstead. The footpaths are in good condition and after a gentle rise into the foothills of the Hertfordshire Chilterns, the only ascents are in and out of a dry valley encountered on the outward and inward routes. At the appropriate season of the year the carpets of bluebells in Berrybushes Wood have to be seen to be believed.

KINGS LANGLEY to The Cart and Horses, Commonwood.

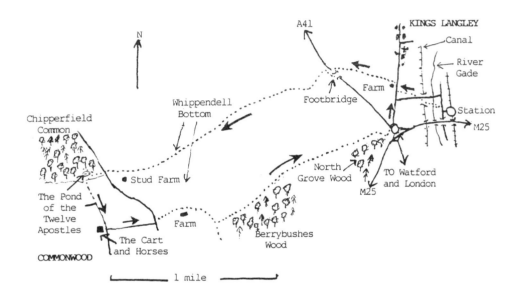

KINGS LANGLEY lies in the valley of the River Gade (pronounced Gad), a tributary of the Colne, which in turn is a tributary of the Thames. The Gade's water are conducive to paper making and paper mills are a feature of the valley. Close by the river are the waters of the Grand Union Canal, threading its way through many locks on its way to Birmingham. The old village lies some three-quarters of a mile north of the station, and remains comparatively unspoiled, and quieter nowadays, as the old trunk road, the A41 has been diverted to the west.

Leaving the station exit, cross the road, and go right for a few paces, and then turn left along an alley with some industrial buildings on your right. After crossing the river and the canal, cross over the road to a footpath sign opposite, and bear left along this old lane to emerge into the main road in some 150 yards. Here turn right. Cross the road where there are farm buildings on the left, and go through the farmyard, and over a stile to follow a clear track which rises with the hedge on the right. Eventually one comes to the fencing of the re-routed A41 road. Cross a stile in the fencing, and bear left to a footbridge. On leaving the bridge turn right and at a stile a little way ahead, go slightly more than sharp left (about 100°) and follow a faint path across a field to a stile some 80 yards from its far left-hand corner.

After crossing the stile the path soon joins a hedge on your left. The way lies straight ahead with the path becoming enclosed at places and descends to a substantial 'dip'. This is . . .

WHIPPENDELL BOTTOM, a long dry valley which is a common factor in the 'dip' slope of the Chiltern Hills. It is said that if you descended the valley for five miles or so you would end up in the middle of Watford High Street! The story may be apochryphal and any attempt to 'prove the point' would turn out to be fruitless, because not all of the 'bottom' is a right of way, and quite apart from that, progress would be effectively blocked by the ubiquitous M25 motorway.

Leave the valley by the path which rises steeply with the hedge on the right. Having crossed several stiles, with the buildings of a stud farm on the left, you emerge into a road, which cross to enter the woods of Chipperfield Common. Cross a horse ride and follow the clear track ahead. You soon arrive at . . .

THE POND OF THE TWELVE APOSTLES, a small sheet of shallow

water, surrounded by twelve pollarded lime trees. Neighbouring bench seats make this quiet corner a delightful place to linger.

To the left of the pond is a stile. Cross this to an enclosed path which soon leads into a tiny road. A short way ahead and on the right-hand side is . . .

THE CART AND HORSES at COMMONWOOD, the latter being more of a 'locality' than a village. Remote from through routes and part of the parish of Flaunden, it is just a scattering of dwellings, including the Cart and Horses. Situated as it is at a junction of minor roads, the bar areas which are ample enough are dwarfed by the substantial beer garden. A good variety of food is served in a friendly atmosphere, and cask ales include Marston's Pedigree, Benskins Best Bitter, and Wadsworth's 6X.

Leaving the pub, follow the road ahead, Quickmoor Lane. At the ensuing T-junction, go left and after some 50 yards right along a concreted farm drive. Where the drive enters the farm keep ahead along the clear track that descends into Whippendell Bottom. Follow the valley for a couple of hundred yards to a point where substantial woods loom up on the hillside on the left. Turn left, ascending quite steeply to join the left-hand margin of the wooded ground. The way ahead becomes simple – just keep straight on with

51

the woods on the right, and after a mile descend steps to the A41 trunk road. Great care and patience are needed to cross this busy highway. Having done so follow the A4251 (the old A41) for 1/4 mile and take the first turning on the right* to the canal bridge and alley encountered on the outward route.

---

* *Those wishing to first visit the taverns, etc. of Kings Langley village keep along the A4251 for ½ mile to the village centre.*

Walk 8

BOXMOOR (Hemel Hempstead Station) to 'the Bull' BOVINGDON and back

BY RAIL . . . Hemel Hempstead station is on the main railway line from London (Euston), Harrow and Wealdstone, and Watford Junction to Leighton Buzzard, Bletchley, Milton Keynes and Northampton. At least two trains per hour on weekdays and Bank Holidays, at least one an hour on Sundays.

BY ROAD . . . From M1, Junction 8 and through Hemel Hempstead town centre to Boxmoor. Alternatively from M25, Junction 20 south of Kings Langley and thence by A4251.

MAP . . . Ordnance Survey Landranger Sheet 166.

DISTANCE OF WALK . . . Approximately 5½ miles.

TOPOGRAPHY . . . Between the headwaters of the River Gade at Hemel Hempstead, and of the River Chess at Chesham lies a corner of the Chiltern Hills which does not attain heights of much more than 400 feet, but the feeling of being 'high up' are apparent, particularly on a breezy day. There are some dry valleys, an example of which is met towards the end of the outward walk to Bovingdon. The area is remote from 'ribbon development'. Underfoot, the going is reasonable at all times of the year. The area is particularly attractive in spring when bluebells adorn the hedgerows and in autumn when the trees in the wooded grounds turn to gold. You will need to have an average degree of fitness to ascend the steep slopes at the beginning of the ramble, but once the heights have been attained, nothing daunting follows. Apart from Bovingdon, refreshments can be obtained at two inns in the close vicinity of Boxmoor station.

BOXMOOR (Hemel Hempstesd Station) to "THE Bull", BOVINGDON

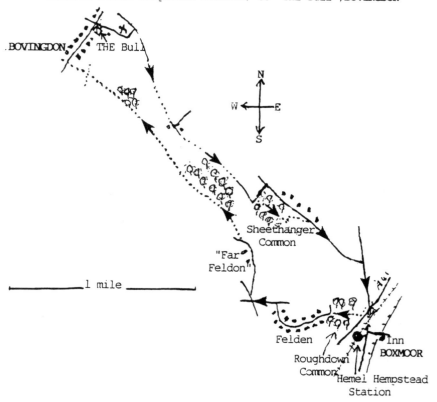

Leave Hemel Hempstead Station and go left through the station approach to join the main road. The locality that you are in is . . .

BOXMOOR, which was a hamlet around meadows through which flow the waters of the Grand Union Canal on its tortuous journey from London to Birmingham. It now forms the southern extremity of the satellite town of Hemel Hempstead. The railway station was formerly known as Boxmoor (for Hemel Hemsptead) and lies almost two miles distant from the centre of the latter. Ironically when 'Hemel' (as it is affectionately known) was a smallish country market town, it had a station right in the town centre. Rationalisation of the railway system caused this to be closed – a year or so later it was decreed that 'Hemel' would become a gigantic 'overspill' town, and so it became – minus the town centre trains. Such is 20th century life! It is refreshing to note that parts of the old line have been converted into a countryfied 'cycleway'.

Follow the main road for a short way passing under arches, and immediately after the last of the arches, go very sharp left on to a path which for a little way runs parallel to a new road on your left, and then veers half right ascending very steeply (including some steps) through the trees of . . .

ROUGHDOWN COMMON, a steeply wooded hillside, now sadly bisected by the re-routed A41 trunk road, which cuts a chalky swath hereabouts.

Keeping straight the path leads into the metalled surface of a private road, which notwithstanding is a public right of way for pedestrians. Follow this road between opulent properties coming eventually to a T-junction with a public road where turn to the left. The neighbourhood in which you are now is . . .

FELDEN, a hilltop settlement around a meeting of minor roads including the aforementioned properties. No sign of commerce or industry pervades the peace of the area, but its denizens can console themselves that the shopping malls of modern 'Hemel' are only some ten minutes away by car or taxicab.

A couple of hundred yards or so ahead you come to a cross roads. Here turn right, and after a few paces go again rightwards where the road forks. The ensuing narrow tarred lane passes large houses on the left-hand side. After going by the entrance to a house called Far Felden, the lane veers sharply to the left. Here go ahead along a footpath which soon leads through a substantial gap in the hedge ahead, and keeping a straight course here edges towards the right-hand side of the field, continuing thereafter with woods on your right. At the end of this field negotiate a stile and carry on in a forward direction with the hedge on the right. The path leads on through this large field, down into a dip, with a spinney on the right, and uphill out of the dip to a crossing of paths at the far right-hand corner of the field. Keep forward again here, the path now running a short way from the hedge on your left. At the end of this field, the path becomes enclosed and after a few yards emerges into a road on the outskirts of ...

BOVINGDON, an airy, but somewhat suburbanised village on high ground. West of the village, there was an airfield, but the buildings associated with this are now used as a penal establishment. The attractive parish church is passed as you leave the village on the return walk.

Turn right on reaching the road, descending gently, and in a short ¼ mile reaching on your right ...

THE BULL public house, an attractive and homely inn with separate public and saloon bars. Good bar snacks are available, and cask ales include Benskins Best Bitter. This ale, when it was brewed at Watford was ubiquitous in this part of the Chilterns. Years ago, this same brewery supplied an alternative cask ale known as 'light mild' –

it was pleasant and refreshing and not being too 'heady' was a favourite tipple of ramblers and cyclists.

Leaving the Bull turn immediately to the right on a minor road which passes the church on your left. Then turn sharp left round the headland of the churchyard, coming in some 150 yards to a T-junction of minor thoroughfares. Turn right along a bridleway dubbed on a notice as being 'unsuitable for motor vehicles'. Follow this delightful backwater for some 1½ miles until it descends into a valley, and turns sharp left. Having negotiated the turn to the left go off along a path that goes half right into the woods. The clear path winds amongst the trees and soon descends steeply into a valley. This delightful tract of hilly woodland is . . .

SHEETHANGER COMMON a largely unspoiled area bounded on its north-western wide by the 'B' road that leads from Boxmoor up through a valley to Bovingdon.

At the valley bottom go right, still descending. Soon the woods on the right give way to grassland. Go right over the grass and then gradually descend to join the road at the end of the commonland. Follow the road for ¼ mile to an intersection with traffic lights, and here turn right and through the arches where the ramble started and into Hemel Hempstead station yard.

Walk 9

BERKHAMSTED to 'the Plough', POTTEN END and back

BY RAIL . . . Berkhamsted station is on the railway line from London (Euston), Harrow and Wealdstone, and Watford Junction to Leighton Buzzard, Bletchley, Milton Keynes and Northampton. At least 3 trains per hour on weekdays. At least one an hour on Sundays.

BY ROAD . . . From M1 Junction 8 and through Hemel Hempstead to Boxmoor, thence by A4251 to Berkhamsted.

MAP . . . Ordnance Survey Landranger Sheets 165 and 166.

DISTANCE OF WALK . . . Approximately 5¼ miles.

TOPOGRAPHY . . . The slopes north of the town of Berkhamsted lead to a well-wooded tract of quiet countryside bordered on the north-west by the vast woodlands and commons which stretch almost to the escarpment of the Chilterns at Dunstable Downs. The footpaths are all easy to follow and well signposted. Apart from a short sharp rise some three-quarters of a mile from the start of the ramble, and an equally short and sharp ascent on leaving the tiny village of Frithsden, the way is level with the exception of a long descent from Little Heath to the Grand Union Canal in the valley below.

BERKHAMSTED is a pleasant town above the headwaters of a valley in the Chiltern Hills, through which passes the old route of the A41 road which leads from the London area to the Vale of Aylesbury and beyond. The town has become quieter now that the new route of the A41 runs through the hillside to the south. The main 'West Coast' railway to Scotland and the Grand Union Canal share the route through the valley. In recent decades the town has become very

Berkhamsted to The Plough, Potten End, and back.

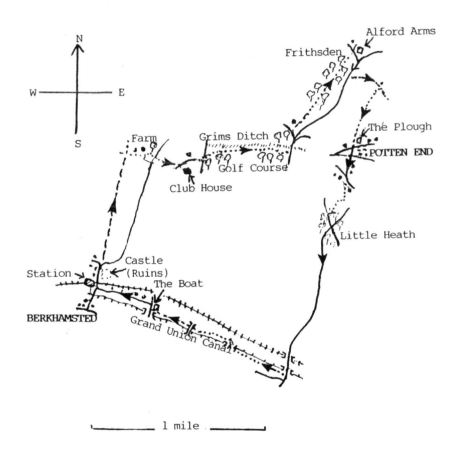

popular with London commuters and developments of new houses abound on the surrounding hillsides.

Leaving the station of the 'up' (north) side go ahead along a local road with the castle ruins on your right. Where the road bears sharply to the left, go forward on to a footpath which after passing through a tarred area continues with the cricket ground on your left. The clear path goes ahead with the hedge on your left. At the last stile before coming to some farm buildings, turn sharp right along a farm track uphill and with the farmhouse on the left. The farm drive turns to the right, and at this point go ahead into a wooded area. The clear path soon veers to the right and in a few yards emerges into a byroad which cross to a bridleway. The way ahead is on a rising gradient, and soon bears leftwards on to a grassy area and joining the driveway of Berkhamsted Golf Club. Carry on along the drive to a T-junction.

Here cross the road and go through a gap in the bushes and then go half left to join in some 50 yards or so a ditch and ridge. This is the course of . . .

GRIM'S DITCH, an earthwork of prehistoric and unknown origin. The ditch is known as the motte and the bank the bailey. Some theories form a conclusion that the ditch had a strategic defensive purpose. Others hold the view that it might have had something to do with keeping unwanted animals away. The earthwork crops up at various points behind the north-west slopes of the Chilterns and may once have attained a length of some 25 miles.

Having joined the ditch continue along its bed for about ¼ mile. Where the way ahead becomes overgrown and by a golf tee on your right take a path which goes slightly rightwards and then veers left to join a road. Here turn left arriving in a couple of hundred yards at a junction of ways. At this point take the private road ahead, Frithsden Copse, and where it bends round to the left keep ahead along a public footpath which soon reaches wooded ground and eventually descends rapidly to join a quiet road by the 'Alford Arms' pub at . . .

FRITHSDEN, a tiny village that nestles picturesquely, almost entirely surrounded by hills. It must be one of the most peaceful spots within a 25 mile radius of central London. It has no shops and no church – just the aforementioned pub, the Alford Arms. It represents the Chiltern country at its very best, yet only a few miles away are the vast acres of the 'overspill' town of Hemel Hempstead. Nothing of

these 'improvements' can be seen from the tranquility of Frithsden.

Passing the pub on your left carry on for a short way to a junction of roads where go right. In a few yards leave the road by turning to the left on to a bridleway which ascends the side of the valley between hedges. After about ¼ mile the way bends distinctly rightwards. Opposite a shed on your left, turn sharp right over a stile and follow the clear path over a second stile and ahead with some lightly wooded ground on your left. The way soon becomes a farm track which leads out into . . .

POTTEN END village, a spread out locality set amongst the higher ground and bordered on its western wide by the vast acres of Berkhamsted Common and the associated open spaces of Ashridge Woods.

As you enter the village, on your left is . . .

THE PLOUGH INN set opposite a green. A variety of cask ales are available together with a good selection of home-cooked food. The inn exudes a very friendly atmosphere and a visit certainly refreshes both the body and the mind for the return walk to Berkhamsted.

Leaving the pub keep forward over the main road with the post office on your right and then straight across a crossroads with a village green now on your right to join another road at a T-junction. Here cross the road to a footpath opposite, which starts its course as a narrow drive to the local bowling club. In some 40 yards and past

the bowlers' entrance the route continues as a really delightful enclosed way. The path is narrow and runs between high hedges. After bending to the right and then to the left, the path emerges into a road where turn right for a few steps and then upon joining another road go left. The woodland with which you are now surrounded is known as . . .

LITTLE HEATH, a small area of wooded commonland, criss-crossed by a couple of minor roads. Excursions off the road and into the woodland indicate by the 'up and down' nature of the terrain, that the area was at one time quarried.

In a hundred yards or so you come to the crossroads in the middle of the heath. Here turn right as signposted to Berkhamsted, and follow the ensuing little road for a good mile, dropping downhill after leaving the woodland, and with lovely views across the valley. Cross a railway bridge and then the canal. Having crossed the latter, descend to the towing path and follow the water side into the environs of Berkhamsted town. (At one of the bridges the towpath changes sides.) At a bridge by a pub, the Boat, ascend from the canal and go right past the front of the pub, and in a few more yards left into Station Road, which in a short ¼ mile leads directly to the station entrance. The High Street and town centre lie a little way to your left.

Walk 10

TRING STATION to 'the White Lion', STARTOPS END (Marsworth) and back

BY RAIL . . . Tring Station is on the main line from London (Euston) via Watford Junction and Hemel Hempstead. From a northerly aspect the railway leads from Northampton through Milton Keynes and Leighton Buzzard. At least two trains per hour on weekdays or Bank Holidays, at least one an hour on Sundays.

BY ROAD . . . Tring is on the A4251 road from the intersection of the M25 and A41 at Kings Langley in the south, and the intersection back to the A41, west of Tring. From Tring town take Station Road (at east end of High Street). From a northerly direction leave the M1 at Junction 11, go through Dunstable town on to B489. Soon turn left along B4506, turning right after some five miles along unclassified road signposted to Aldbury. Tring station is just over a mile beyond Aldbury village.

MAPS . . . Ordnance Survey Pathfinder Sheet 165 or Explorer Sheet 2.

DISTANCE OF WALK . . . Approximately 6 miles.

TOPOGRAPHY . . . The 'Tring Gap' is really a broad valley through the Chiltern Escarpment, some three miles in width. The summit area is in excess of 400 feet above sea level, with a gentle slope of the south-east back to the Gade Valley at Hemel Hempstead. On the north-western aspect the land drops away to the great Vale of Aylesbury which is verily the gateway to the Midlands. The poet, Rupert Brooke writing from a neighbouring height referred to his view northwards as 'The Slumbering Midland Plain'. The walk encounters the scene of great engineering feats of bygone years, when the canal and railway penetrated the gap. The ramble will appeal to those who shun gradients. The whole route does not encounter any substantial ups or downs.

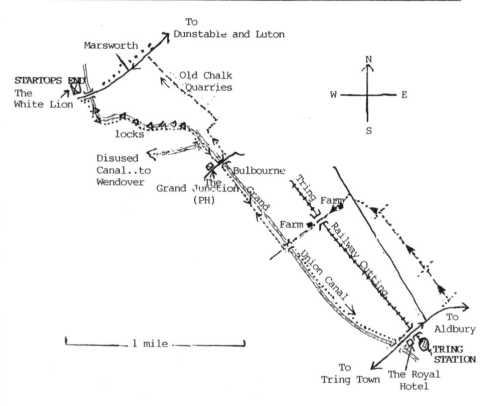

To Dunstable and Luton

Marsworth

STARTOPS END
The
White Lion

Old Chalk Quarries

locks

Disused Canal..to Wendover

Grand Junction The (PH)

Bulbourne

Tring Farm

Farm

Farm

Grand

Union Canal

Railway Cutting

N
W — E
S

1 mile

To Aldbury

TRING STATION

To Tring Town

The Royal Hotel

64

TRING STATION is 'out in the country', situated as it is some 2½ miles from the centre of Tring town. Apart from a row of old cottages, a hotel and a pub, 'the Royal', and a small new but secluded housing development, there is nothing around but the rolling countryside, where the Chiltern ridges give way to the great 'Midland Plain'. Just south of the station the main railway line from London to Birmingham attains its highest altitude.

Leaving the station by the main exit, recross the railway by the road bridge. Ignoring a turning on the left signposted to Pitstone and Ivinghoe, proceed ahead for a short way to a point where the road veers off to the right. Here go ahead on a right of way which begins as a concrete track. Where the concrete way goes left towards some farm buildings go straight on and after some 20 yards through a gate. Here turn left along the 'Ridgeway' long distance path which at this point is in the form of a leafy green lane. The bank to the right is well 'perforated' and the odds are that rabbits will be darting to and fro as you proceed. At a junction of paths go forward and follow a chalky and clear path across a field with wooded ground some few yards to your right.

You soon reach another signposted crossroads of pathways and the way again lies ahead into an enclosed bridleway that in some 400 yards leads out into a by-road. Follow this road for 100 yards, and then turn left down a farm drive which after passing farm buildings goes through a gate and becomes a pleasant green lane. You soon cross the railway. Look over the parapet and you will have a great view either way of . . .

TRING CUTTING, a deep excavation some two miles long.This was one of the great engineering feats during the building last century of the London and Birmingham Railway. It enables the line to descend from the hill country to the vale without severe gradients. In railways terms it became one of the wonders of the world when first opened.

Having crossed the bridge you pass a further farm where the track becomes tarred again. In ¼ mile you go through another gate (look back at the notice on the gate which indicates that the road is private but 'WALKERS WELCOME' – a nice thought). In a few yards you cross the Grand Union Canal by a high bridge. Having crossed the bridge turn right and descend to the canal bank. The deep tree-lined cutting is part of the . . .

SUMMIT POUND of the Grand Union Canal. A pound is the stretch of water between two locks, and in this particular instance the locks at either end take the waterway to a lower level. This waterway cutting is not as deep as its counterpart on the railway, but nevertheless represented another great engineering feat of its day.

Keeping forward by the canal, you come in about three-quarters of a mile to a bridge at the hamlet of . . .

BULBOURNE, reputedly pronounced Boobun by the local fraternity. It consists of a few cottages, a largish boat yard and an attractive pub named the Grand Junction which was the original name of the canal.

Cross the bridge and some 40 yards ahead go left along a bridleway that runs enclosed amongst trees and bushes. In about ¼ mile the path turns sharply to the right and a little further on to the left, continuing now with open views ahead and joining a classified road at the fringe of the village of Marsworth. This road is steeped in antiquity being the . .

ICKNIELD WAY, a pre-Roman highway that ran from East Anglia down to the Thames at the Oxfordshire–Berkshire border. Its name derives from the ancient British Iceni tribe.

Turn left upon joining the road. In an easy ten minutes you are at the canal again at . . .

STARTOPS END, an outpost of nearby Marsworth village. Just a few cottages and a couple of pubs and the canal bridge. One is given to understand that the local pronounciation of the place is 'Starrops End'.

Crossing the bridge you come to the attractive and commodious inn, the . . .

WHITE LION, with ample space to drink and eat both inside and outside. A half dozen different cask ales are available from brewers throughout the country. A wide variety of food is dispayed on blackboards.

Leaving the inn, cross the road and descend to the right-hand bank of the canal. During the next half mile you pass seven locks, then over a bridge across the entrance to the . . .

WENDOVER ARM, a branch of the main canal that tortuously followed the contour of the land to the pretty town of Wendover. Much of its course is now dry and derelict, and sadly to say the site of the old wharf at Wendover has been built over.

Whilst passing the locks you will observe on your right small ponds. These are known as side ponds and are now disused. Their purpose was to conserve water when the locks were emptied for 'downhill' traffic. The lakes (also on your right) are reservoirs to supply the summit level of the waterway with adequate supplies. These expanses of water, three in all, are of great interest to bird watchers.

Soon after passing the last lock you come to Bulbourne Bridge and its adjacent pub, encountered on the outward journey. From here retrace your steps to the the next bridge. Climb up to this and cross it, thence descending to the opposite (left) bank, which follow for a good mile to the next bridge. Here join the road and go left. In a couple of hundred yards you return to Tring Station.

Walk 11

STANSTEAD ST. MARGARETS
(St. Margarets Station*) to 'the White Horse', WARESIDE, and back

BY RAIL . . . From London (Liverpool Street) via Tottenham and Broxbourne. Beyond St. Margarets railway continues to Ware and Hertford (East). Half hourly service weekdays. Hourly on Sundays upon which day you will be obliged to change trains at Broxbourne.

BY ROAD . . . Using A10 trunk road, thence A414 and B181. Access to A10 from M25 is at Junction 25. From M1, leave at Junction 7, thence M10, A414, A10 and B181.

MAP . . . Ordnance Survey Landranger Sheet 166.

DISTANCE OF WALK . . . Approximately 5 miles.

TOPOGRAPHY . . . To the immediate north of the 'industrialised' Lea (or Lee) valley lies a sparsely populated agricultural area inconveniently placed for commuters on account of the only railway line having been closed many years ago. The destination, the tiny village of Wareside is in the valley of the little known River Ash. The stream's main claim to fame is in the nearby village of Much Hadham, with its photogenic watersplash. Hedges are few in these parts – wide open views are the order of the day, the soil a mixture of chalk and reddish clay. The 'going' is normally good for all of the route, except for puddles which obstinately remain in 'dips' long after rain has fallen. A feature of this walk is that there are no stiles to cross, notwithstanding the fact that the bulk of the route is away from public roads.

---

* *If booking a railway ticket from the London Area, be sure to ask for St. Margarets,* HERTS. *There is another St. Margarets in the parish of Twickenham, Middlesex.*

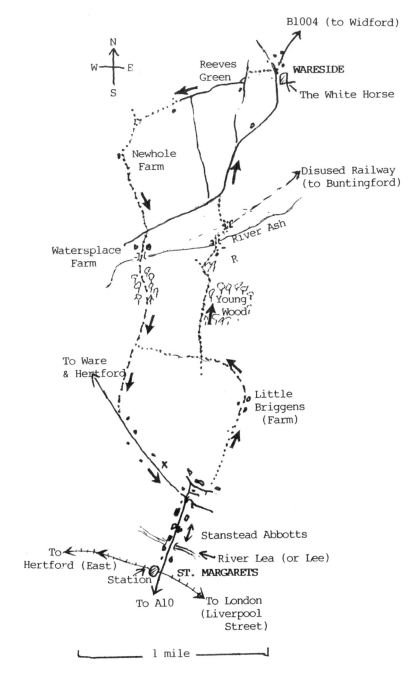

B1004 (to Widford)

N
W—E
S

Reeves
Green

WARESIDE

The White Horse

Newhole
Farm

Disused Railway
(to Buntingford)

River Ash

Watersplace
Farm

R

Young
Wood

To Ware
& Hertford

Little
Briggens
(Farm)

Stanstead Abbotts

To
Hertford (East)

River Lea (or Lee)

Station

ST. MARGARETS

To A10

To London
(Liverpool
Street)

1 mile

ST. MARGARETS is the name of the railway station in the parish of Stanstead St. Margarets. Coming from London the locality marks the end of an almost continual ribbon of domestic and industrial development which borders the lower end of Lea (or Lee) valley.

Leaving the station on the up side, turn left into main street. In a short while you cross the 'Lea Navigation', a substantial waterway which is a mixture of canal and river. Having crossed the bridge you are now at . . .

STANSTEAD ABBOTS, a riverside village much frequented by anglers. The village is a 'frontier area' between the industry to the south and the sparsely populated countryside to its north. During the course of the High Street you will pass three public houses and a cafe.

At the end of the High Street go left for a few yards and crossing the road turn right along a residential road, Cappell Way. Rising quite steeply take the left-hand road at the next junction and continuing uphill for some 30 yards you come to a T-junction. Here turn right. At the end of a row of houses turn left on to a signposted footpath which ascends steps as it quickly gains height. You emerge in open country and aim ahead along the clear track eventually coming to the farm buildings of Little Briggens. Having passed between the buildings the track bears off leftwards and in a good half mile arrives at a signposted crossing of ways. Here turn right. The way ahead tips slightly and then rises eventually skirting some woods on your right. The woods end and shortly a further wood is passed, again on your right. At the end of this little wood leave the main track and go rightwards descending the valley side. In some 75 yards you pass a solitary house on your right. At this point there is a junction of ways. Keep ahead along a narrow path which after a few steps crosses the River Ash by a footbridge.

Continue on a forward direction at this point and soon the path veers slightly rightwards. On your immediate left now is the course of an abandoned railway line. (This ran from St. Margarets to the town of Buntingford before it fell under 'the Beeching Axe' – the absence of any commuter line hereabouts has led to the area being so sparsely populated.) Going slightly uphill, in a few yards on you turn left over the 'railway' bridge. Having crossed this, turn immediately to your right along a clear path which slants uphill to join a road. Go forward in this road and in some ½ mile you will descend to the centre of the village of . . .

WARESIDE in a sort of 'sleepy hollow' with the meadows of the tiny River Ash to the east, and low hills to the west, in which a matter of some three miles away lies the remote hamlet with the picturesque name of Cold Christmas! The road (B1004) which passes through Wareside is something of a byeway itself being a cross-country link between the towns of Ware and Bishops Stortford.

As you enter Wareside, on your right is . . .

THE WHITE HORSE, a rural establishment with a separate public bar. The well-known East Anglian brewers, Greene King, supply the beers, the low gravity version being IPA (India Pale Ale) and the stronger the renowned Abbott Ale. Greene King also took over and closed Rayments Brewery which operated from the rural village of Furneux Pelham, but still brew a Rayments Bitter, a slightly sweeter brew than IPA, but extremely palatable. The White Horse have a varied menu of meals and bar snacks to suit all tastes.

Leaving the White Horse cross the road to an intersection of roads. In the corner on your left is a little alley which soon leads into a delightful 'enclosed way' accompanied on your left by a substantial ditch. In a short ¼ mile you emerge into a minor road at Reeves Green where turn left for a few paces and then right. The tiny lane that you are now traversing does not lead to anywhere in particular. In a matter of 500 yards the lane bends off to your right.

Keep forward here along a small road signposted 'road used as a public footpath'. You soon pass between the buildings of Morley Hall veering firstly leftward and then rightwards as you do so. The route then peters out and becomes an enclosed green lane, soon descending to a point where there is a picturesque 'triangular junction' with a similar green way. Keeping leftwards you rise out of a dip, pass a farm and continue along a 'made up' farm drive and then back to the B1004. Cross this 'highway' to another farm drive opposite.

The return route is the essence of simplicity hereon. The drive passes a farm, crosses the river by a footbridge by a ford, rises through a woodland glade and continues on in delightfully rural surroundings to eventually descend in the form of a track to join a road. In short, once you have crossed the B1004 you just carry on ignoring all tracks, etc., to the right or left. On eventually emerging into the road keep forward to join the outward route at the junction at the end of Stanstead Abbots High Street which traverse back to St. Margarets station.

Walk 12

WATTON AT STONE to 'the Horns', BULLS GREEN and back

BY RAIL . . . Watton at Stone station is on a 'loop line' from Alexander Palace in North London to Stevenage. On weekdays London trains normally leave from Moorgate. Connections from London (Kings Cross) and from the underground systems are available at Finsbury Park. At weekends trains usually run direct from Kings Cross to Watton At Stone, service hourly weekdays or Sundays.

BY ROAD . . . From London area, A10 (Cambridge) road passing Junction 25 of M25. Whilst on Ware by-pass take left-hand turn at junction with A602 which leads in some four miles to Watton at Stone. From other directions aim for Hertford town and thereafter follow A119 in a northerly direction.

MAP . . . Ordnance Survey Landranger Sheet 166.

DISTANCE OF WALK . . . Approximately 5 miles.

TOPOGRAPHY . . . The eastern side of the county of Hertfordshire bears an East Anglian flavour with many roads unfenced and unhedged. The subsoil bears a 'Chiltern' flavour with chalky tracts mixed with flint and pockets of clay, the latter often being of a pinkish hue. The route is mainly of a gentle rising nature on the way to Bulls Green, the one major exception being the substantial dip encountered after the end of the first mile. No villages or hamlets are passed on either the outward or inward routes. This is quiet country which belies its proximity to neighbouring industrial towns. Muddy after rain? Yes, the bridle paths in particular tend to hold moisture! Refreshments before or after the ramble are available by making the brief diversion to Watton village centre. There is no 'Railway Tavern' in the vicinity of the station.

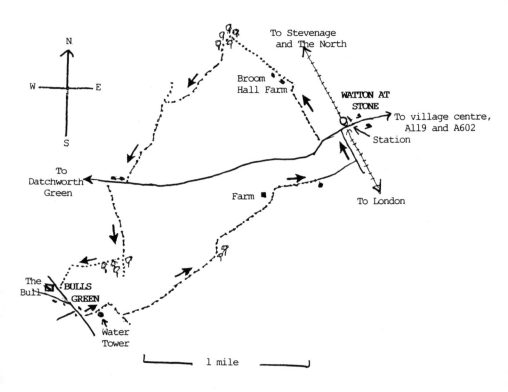

To Stevenage
and The North

N

W —+— E

S

Broom
Hall Farm

WATTON AT
STONE

To village centre,
A119 and A602

Station

To
Datchworth
Green

Farm

To London

The
Bull

BULLS
GREEN

Water
Tower

1 mile

WATTON AT STONE is a quiet and comparatively unspoiled village situated midway between the county town of Hertford and the sprawling 'new town' of Stevenage. It lies in a shallow valley of the River Beane, a tributary of the Lee (or Lea). The village centre is some ¼ mile to the east of the railway station. The station itself is something of a reinstatement. For many years after the 'Beeching Era', the line was closed except for freight or diverted trains and the old station became derelict. Common sense eventually prevailed and when the line was electrified a new, albeit austere station was built and passenger services resumed. Apart from a 'rash' of new housing development adjacent to the 'up' platform the locality is rural, so much so that immediately you cross the bridge across the line you are in open country.

Having left the station and crossed the bridge follow the road to a point where on your right is a gravelled farm track. Turn right along the track and continue to a point at which are farm buildings on your immediate right. Having passed the buildings ignore the continuation of the gravelled way and go right along a grassy way which very soon leads out into a tarred farm road, where turn left. The road soon peters out and here you keep straight ahead into a substantial dip and up the other side to reach a belt of wooded ground. On entering the trees turn left and follow the bridleway through the narrow belt of trees and thereafter into a huge field. Cross this field in a forward direction to a point near the far boundary where the path veers slightly to the right to join another track where turn left.

In some ½ mile this track emerges into a secondary road. Here turn right. After a short ¼ mile and where a side road comes in from your right, turn left along a rough track. After approximately half a mile you descend into a slight dip, soon reaching wooded ground. At a point immediately before the woods start turn right and follow a path on the left-hand side of a large field. You will eventually see a pond on your left and just after passing this look out for a concealed stile. Turn left and cross the stile and continue along the left-hand side of the meadow. When the hedge bends left keep forward and emerge from the meadow by way of a further stile adjoining a bungalow. Here turn right in the road to emerge on . . .

BULLS GREEN, one of several 'greens' which abound in this area.

It is a meeting place of minor roads with a scattering of dwellings and a rural looking garage.

Cross the green and facing you is . . .

THE HORNS, a classic example of an English pub on a village green. A pity that the green is not big enough for a game of cricket – that would complete the rural scene. Several cask ales are available and a selection of traditional bar snacks. There are south facing beer tables in the front of the building. Situated as it is only a few miles from industrial Welwyn Garden City and 'modernised' Stevenage it is a place to linger at. Only the quietest of minor roads lead to the locality.

Leaving the pub retrace your steps for a short way and where you emerged from the stile by the bungalow keep ahead on the minor road. Take the left-hand route at the junction of roads and after some 100 yards you come to a place where unmade tracks lead leftwards. Take the right-hand branch of these tracks soon passing a covered reservoir and a water tower on your right. Where the fencing on your right ends turn right along a clear and rutted bridleway. At a slight dip and approaching some bushes turn left along a clear track which traverses another huge field. Hereafter the return route is as simple as it is rural. Just follow the track on passing a clump of trees on the right (the site of an old quarry). The way veers left and then right and later through a gate with a farm on your left, through another gate past a cottage whereabouts the way becomes tarred. You emerge at a T-junction where turn left. In less than a quarter of a mile you are back at the bridge by Watton at Stone station.

Walk 13

BRICKET WOOD to 'the Round Bush', ROUND BUSH (Aldenham) and back

BY RAIL . . . Bricket Wood station is on the branch line from Watford Junction. Connections to the main London–Watford–Hemel Hempstead–Leighton Buzzard–Milton Keynes line twice to the hour weekdays, once on Sundays. Beyond Bricket Wood trains run to and from the tiny station of St. Albans (Abbey).

BY ROAD . . . Bricket Wood is accessible from the main Watford–St. Albans road (A405) midway between Junction 21a of the M25 and Junction 6 of the M1. An unclassified road leads in a south-easterly direction for the three-quarter mile diversion to Bricket Wood.

MAP . . . Ordnance Survey Landranger Sheet 166.

DISTANCE OF WALK . . . Approximately 5¾ miles.

TOPOGRAPHY . . . Between the urban sprawl of present day Watford and the expanding city of St. Albans lies a surprisingly peaceful tract of unspoiled country bordering the valley of the River Colne. The only reminder that you are close to 'civilisation' comes at a point some 1¾ miles on the outward route when from a gentle upland prior to crossing the Colne you can, if visibility permits, see the buildings centred around Watford High Street. The underfoot conditions are mainly clay which becomes sticky after rain. The final part of the walk over Bricket Wood Common can in places be decidedly 'boggy'. Substantial waterproof footwear is the order of the day, particularly in winter and spring.

BRICKET WOOD is something of a suburb of Watford. Amongst deeply wooded country, residential properties were built this century between the main A405 (Watford to St. Albans) road and the little

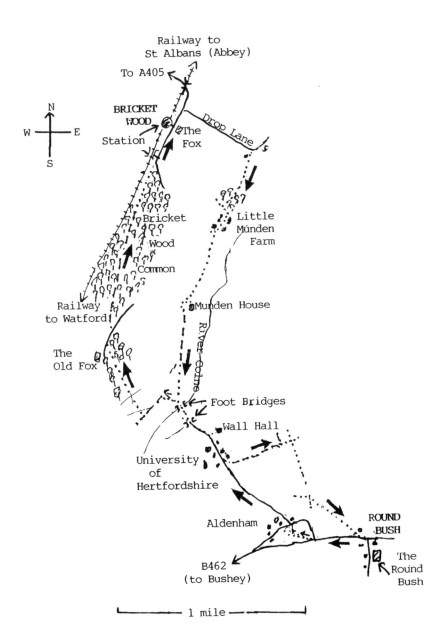

Railway to
St Albans (Abbey)

To A405

N
W — E
S

BRICKET
WOOD
Station

The
Fox

Drop Lane

Little
Múnden
Farm

Bricket
Wood
Common

Múnden House

River Colne

Railway
to Watford

The
Old Fox

Foot Bridges

Wall Hall

University
of
Hertfordshire

ROUND
BUSH

Aldenham

The
Round
Bush

B462
(to Bushey)

└──── 1 mile ──·──┘

single line branch railway which links these same towns. On the eastern side of the locality the railway line became a frontier post between rural and suburban Hertfordshire.

Leaving the station forecourt opposite the Fox public house turn left. In some 150 yards turn right along Drop Lane (even at this early stage of the walk you are in the heart of the countryside). Follow this narrow thoroughfare for almost ½ mile and just before it takes a sharp turn to the left turn right across a stile and follow a path which runs between a barn and a hedge. Where the hedge veers off to the left keep ahead soon picking up a line of wooded ground on your left. At the far corner of the field the path keeps its straight course entering the woods and shortly descending first gradually and then quite steeply to a stile. Cross this and then over a narrow field to another stile out into a farm drive where turn left.

Continue between the farm buildings and where these end on your left go over a stile and then another, this time into a large field. The path takes a slightly rightwards course rising gently as it does so. Aim for a point to the right of a large house seen ahead and emerge from this field into a drive and continue with the precincts of the house on your left, and keeping forward out into a driveway through parkland. In some ¼ mile the driveway takes a slight turn to the right. As the guidepost informs you the footpath lies ahead. This clear path soon descends slightly and leads to a substantial footbridge over the . . .

RIVER COLNE, a tributary of the Thames into which it flows in the neighbourhood of Staines. On its way it passes through Watford, Rickmansworth, Uxbridge and a point just westwards of the runways of Heathrow Airport. In the lower reaches some of the flow is diverted to the artificial Longford River* which nowadays runs below the airport *en route* to Hampton Court Palace, its original purpose being to supply the palace with water.

Having crossed the bridge the clear path leads diagonally leftwards to another (somewhat vertigo inspiring) high and humpbacked wooden footbridge over a 'flood channel' which is normally dry. There is as an alternative a ford to the right-hand side of the footbridge. Ignoring a footpath which goes off to your left keep forward and slightly uphill along the gravelly track and via a gate and stile out into the campus of . . .

---

* *Also known as the Duke of Northumberland's River.*

THE UNIVERSITY OF HERTFORDSHIRE, which amongst the modern conglomeration of 'outbuildings' contains (on your left) the fine old castellated house, Wall Hall, built around 1830.

Keeping ahead and rising gently through the campus you come to a point where the main drive veers off to your right. Here go slightly left following a sign which amongst other things guides you to the day nursery. (Such modern 'cons' they have nowadays at these places of learning.) Then having passed the nursery on your left the campus is left behind. The way becomes a field track which after a short ¼ mile takes a sharp turn to the left. Here go straight on with the hedge on your left for about 30 yards where there is a meeting place of footpaths. Go sharp right here with the hedge again on your left. In the next field you come to another meeting of public footpaths and here you go left over a stile. The path runs ahead and diagonally over the next field with a line of pylons veering slightly away to your left. A stile leads into the next field which is used for soccer and rugby, etc., being the grounds of a nearby private boarding school. In the far left-hand corner of the field and adjacent to the school drive you emerge into a 'B' classified road. Cross this and in a few yards turn to the right. You are at the verge of the hamlet of . . .

ROUND BALL, a locality which is eponymous with the local pub having grown around it. Better known examples of this sort of thing are found in the London area, e.g. Angel, Elephant and Castle, etc.

Having turned right, on your left is . . .

THE ROUND BALL public house in a rural setting down the secondary road that leads to nearby Letchmore Heath. As is common nowadays the 'one bar' system applies but the resulting commodious area contains pleasant alcoves in which to sit and enjoy the drinks and food. Of the former one of the available cask ales is Benskins (formerly of Watford) best bitter. Of the latter there is a varied selection of snacks and sandwiches.

Leaving the pub retrace your steps to the 'B' road and turn left. In a short while a turning comes in on the right. Do not turn sharp right into this by-road but instead (between roads) follow a green way which after some 150 yards emerges in the churchyard and in front of the church into the village of . . .

ALDENHAM, a charmingly rural setting around a green. Incredible it is to contemplate that less than three miles away are the

retail megaliths of Watford's shopping area. Fortunate too that the projected extension of the London Underground system to nearby Bushey Heath was never completed. Had this project materialised the surroundings of Aldenham village would doubtless have become 'suburbanised'. As matters are peace reigns; indeed no through traffic enters the village as in pre-war times a short 'cut off' was built for the benefit of those using the Radlett to Bushey B462 road. An unusual feature of Aldenham is the absence of a village pub – you just have to travel the ¼ mile to (the) Round Bush to partake of your fancy!

On leaving the churchyard turn to your right and then in some 30 yards go leftwards along a road signposted 'public footpath to Bricket Wood'. This road soon assumes its position as the driveway to the university campus which you enter at the intersection with the route to the day nursery. Hereon retrace your steps through the campus and down the lane and over the footbridges. Having crossed the second bridge leave your outward route by going half left along a clear path which ascends slightly and soon joins a drive. Turn left along the drive and after a short way go right on to a footpath which crosses a field with wire fencing on your right. At the end of the field the path enters . . .

BRICKET WOOD COMMON, a substantial area of mainly densely wooded terrain. There is an abundance of silver birch in these woods, this variety of tree being common around swampy areas which abound. It is also said that rare types of fungi can be found hereabouts.

Entering the woods of the common take the path which leads straight ahead. Soon you emerge into a minor road at a clearing with the rural setting of the Old Fox public house a few yards away on your left. Cross the road and after a few yards fork left across the greensward on to a signposted path which runs in front of a few houses at the perimeter of the commonland. Continuing on you pass another dwelling on your right and then you are back on the commonland proper again. The path hereabouts takes a right turn and then immediately sharp left. From here go absolutely straight ahead for nearly a mile ignoring paths to the left and right. (At the 'cross paths' towards the end of this mile a sign indicates that the right of way goes left, but have no reservations, you are on commonland and the forward way is quite negotiable, although somewhat overgrown and rutted.)

At the end of the track you emerge at a junction of minor roads with an arch under the railway on your left. Do not pass under the arch but keep ahead soon coming to the station approach and the Fox Inn.

Walk 14

HARPENDEN to 'the Bull', WHEATHAMSTEAD and back

BY RAIL . . . Harpenden station is on the 'Thameslink' line linking Brighton in the south with Bedford in the north, passing *en route* Croydon, London Bridge, Kings Cross (Thameslink), St. Albans and Luton. Harpenden station lies intermediately between St. Albans and Luton. Usually four trains per hour weekdays, two on Sundays.

BY ROAD . . . Harpenden is on the A1081 (Luton to St. Albans) road. This can be approached from the south via the A6 and St. Albans city centre. Alternatively from M1 at Junction 10, this being viable whether arriving from north or south.

MAP . . . Ordnance Survey Landranger Sheet 166.

DISTANCE OF WALK . . . Approximately 6½ miles.

TOPOGRAPHY . . . East of the valley of the River Lea hereabouts there lies a tract of undulating countryside mainly devoted to the growing of corn. Wide vistas open out amongst the large fields. The river valley itself in this vicinity is mostly unspoiled. Wheathamstead village lies right in the valley but the whole walk is free of steep gradients, the only exception being a short sharp rise of only a few yards. It is perhaps a trifle unfortunate that the walk begins and ends with some three-quarters of a mile of suburban development, but this is unavoidable, as the town has developed on its eastern side, due to the fact that there was another railway station in the valley, but this met its demise under the axe of Dr. Beeching. It so transpires that on the return walk, you use the old railway track for some distance where it has been converted into a delightful by-way under an umbrella of shrubs and trees. A highlight of the route is the tiny hamlet of Mackerye End, so beloved by the famous essayist, Charles Lamb.

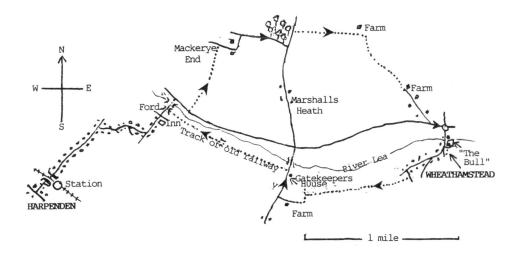

N

W —— E

S

Mackerye
End

Farm

Farm

Ford

Marshalls
Heath

Inn

Track of old railway

River Lea

"The
Bull"

Station

Gatekeepers
House

WHEATHAMSTEAD

HARPENDEN

Farm

⌐_____ 1 mile _____⌐

85

HARPENDEN is a pleasant and even to this day a 'countryfied' town situated almost midway between St. Albans and Luton. The southern end of the High Street abuts on to a substantial tract of commonland. In Station Road where this ramble begins lies a large area of good class housing which stretches down to the eastern end of the town in the river valley.

Leaving Harpenden station turn right into Station Road (the High Street and town centre are a hundred yard or so to your left). The road rises and then begins to fall. Take a turning on the right called Lyndhurst Drive. A way further on you come to a fork, where go leftwards along Granby Avenue. This leads to a T-junction with Craven Lane where turn left, descending over a bridge over an old railway line (more about that later) past the Marquis of Granby pub on the right and straight on across a footbridge beside a ford. This is . . .

RIVER LEA (or LEE), a chalk stream which rises near the appropriately named Leagrave just north of Luton. Having successfully negotiated the industrial centre of the latter, it pursues a peaceful course to where we are standing and thereafter through Welwyn, Hertford and Ware, then taking a mainly southerly course into North East London, through Hackney Marshes joining the Thames in London's East End (perhaps now more correctly known as Docklands!).

After crossing the river, the way soon leads out into a busy road, where go right. Some 200 yards ahead up a rising gradient, turn left along a path which is partly enclosed, with wire fencing on your left and young trees on your right. After a brief incursion for a few yards into the field the path curves back into the camouflage of the fence and the greenery. When the path ends at a tiny road, turn right. Ahead on your left is a mansion, on your right is a farmhouse. This is . . .

MACKERYE END, a scattered hamlet with a magnificent mansion on your left and a farmhouse on the right. The latter was visited by Charles Lamb. In his 'Essays of Elia' he described Mackerye End as 'the oldest thing I remember'. When he revisited the farm many years later he enjoyed walking across the fields to Wheathamstead, possibly taking the same route as we are.

The road bears sharp left (with a magnificent view of the mansion on your left) and soon comes to a T-junction where go to the left. The road, Marshalls Heath Lane, rises and after some 250 yards, turn right on to a bridleway, which crosses a field through a substantial 'dip'. Ahead, the way into the next field is via a steep pitch, only a few yards long with a strip of wooded ground on your right. Having negotiated this short sharp rise the way lies straight ahead. Nearing farm buildings, you are joined by a farm track from the right. Just before the track that you are on veers left into the farm, go sharp right along another track that gradually descends for a good half mile to more farm buildings. Here ignore a footpath which leads over a stile ahead, and follow the farm drive which leads out into a secondary road. Cross this road and keep ahead for a few yards to a roundabout. Here turn right into the village of . . .

WHEATHAMSTEAD, a village in the Lea Valley, which notwithstanding 'progress' retains much of its rural character. The High Street which rises in the direction of Nomansland Common is largely unspoiled. On the south side expansion has taken place in the form of a 'dormitory area', in spite of the fact that the railway and its station were 'axed' by Dr Beeching in the sixties. It is now connected to St. Albans by a reasonably frequent omnibus service, reputed to connect therefrom to fast rail services to the City.

On entering the village keep to the right-hand side of the road and traverse an attractive alley which for a few yards is bordered by a swift and attractive mill stream, and bridging the river, soon emerging back into the main street. On your immediate right is . . .

THE BULL INN, a seventeenth century building that at one time served as the village post office. The pub is now owned by the Beefeater chain, and sports a restaurant in addition to a good variety of reasonably priced bar snacks to suit all tastes. Accommodation is commodious, service is friendly. The only facility lacking is a beer garden – the outside seating is a concreted area. A choice of three cask ales is available, from well-known brewers in the Midlands and the North West.

Leaving the Bull, cross the High Street, and continue ahead with the parish church on your right. An interesting feature here across the road is what was a pub, and still sporting its inn sign. the latter indicates that the building is an Oriental Takeaway – signs of our changing times and tastes! Take the first turning to your right and after some 75 yards where the road forks, go rightwards, along a residential road. Then take the first turning on the left, and after a few yards, right on to a footpath which starts off as being enclosed and then soon emerging into a field which cross to a gap into a second field, where the hedge is on your right and the path gradually veers away from the hedgerow, the 'gap' into the next field is some 30 yards from the far right-hand corner of the field. In the third field the path keeps ahead on the same forward course eventually arriving at a cross path at the end of the field. Here turn left, the ensuing track soon veering round to the right. Continue through farm buildings and follow the lane to a junction with a minor road where go right. The lane descends, and just before a humped bridge over the river is a house on your right. Just past the house in the hedge on your right you will see the remains of a level crossing gate, opposite this gate turn left along a bridleway which follows the former course of the . . .

LONDON AND NORTH EASTERN RAILWAY, this particular line running from what we now call the East Coast Main Line, at Welwyn Garden City, through Harpenden, Luton (Bute Street Station), Dunstable, and across the Vale of Aylesbury to join the London Midland and Scottish Railway (now known as the West Coast Main Line) at Leighton Buzzard. The route is derelict. Now that passenger trains have been reintroduced to Mansfield in Notts., Dunstable must rank as qualifier for the largest town in the U.K. without a railway station.

Follow along the line of the track for a full mile until you come to an overbridge. Ascend to the road above. You are back in Crabtree Lane where you reverse the outgoing route via Granby Avenue, Lyndhurst Drive, and Station Road back to Harpenden station.

# INDEX
W = Walk Number

Books Published by
THE BOOK CASTLE

JOURNEYS INTO BEDFORDSHIRE: Anthony Mackay.
Foreword by The Marquess of Tavistock, Woburn Abbey.
A lavish book of over 150 evocative ink drawings.

A PILGRIMAGE IN HERTFORDSHIRE: H. M. Alderman.
Classic, between-the-wars tour round the county, embellished
with line drawings.

**COUNTRYSIDE CYCLING IN BEDFORDSHIRE,
Buckinghamshire and Hertfordshire:** Mick Payne.
Twenty rides on- and off-road for all the family.

**PUB WALKS FROM COUNTRY STATIONS:
Bedfordshire and Hertfordshire:** Clive Higgs.
Fourteen circular country rambles, each starting and finishing
at a railway station and incorporating a pub-stop at a mid-way
point.

LOCAL WALKS: South Bedfordshire and North Chilterns:
Vaughan Basham. Twenty-seven thematic circular walks.

LOCAL WALKS: North and Mid-Bedfordshire:
Vaughan Basham. Twenty-five thematic circular walks.

FAMILY WALKS: Chilterns South: Nick Moon.
Thirty 3 to 5 mile circular walks.

**CHILTERN WALKS: Hertfordshire, Bedfordshire and
North Buckinghamshire:** Nick Moon.
CHILTERN WALKS: Buckinghamshire: Nick Moon.
**CHILTERN WALKS: Oxfordshire and
West Buckinghamshire:** Nick Moon.
A trilogy of circular walks, in association with the Chiltern
Society. Each volume contains thirty circular walks.

**OXFORDSHIRE WALKS:
Oxford, the Cotswolds and the Cherwell Valley:** Nick Moon.
**OXFORDSHIRE WALKS:
Oxford, the Downs and the Thames Valley:** Nick Moon.
Two volumes that complement Chiltern Walks: Oxfordshire
and complete coverage of the county, in association with the
Oxford Fieldpaths Society. Thirty circular walks in each.

FOLK: Characters and Events in the History of Bedfordshire and Northamptonshire: Vivienne Evans. Anthology about people of yesteryear – arranged alphabetically by village or town.

LEGACIES: Tales and Legends of Bedfordshire and Hertfordshire: Vic Lea. Twenty-five mysteries and stories based on fact, including Luton Town Football Club. Many photographs.

HISTORIC FIGURES IN THE BUCKINGHAMSHIRE LANDSCAPE: John Houghton. Major personalities and events that have shaped the county's past, including a special section on Bletchley Park.

MANORS and MAYHEM, PAUPERS and POLITICS: Tales from Four Shires: Beds., Bucks., Herts., and Northants.: John Houghton. Little-known historical snippets and stories.

MYTHS and WITCHES, PEOPLE and POLITICS: Tales from Four Shires: Bucks., Beds., Herts., and Northants.: John Houghton. Anthology of strange but true historical events.

ECCENTRICS and VILLAINS, HAUNTINGS and HEROES: Tales from Four Shires: Northants., Beds., Bucks., and Herts.: John Houghton. True incidents and curious events covering one thousand years.

DUNSTABLE WITH THE PRIORY, 1100–1550: Vivienne Evans. Dramatic growth of Henry I's important new town around a major crossroads.

DUNSTABLE DECADE: THE EIGHTIES: A Collection of Photographs: Pat Lovering. A souvenir book of nearly 300 pictures of people and events in the 1980s.

DUNSTABLE IN DETAIL: Nigel Benson. A hundred of the town's buildings and features, plus town trail map.

OLD DUNSTABLE: Bill Twaddle. A new edition of this collection of early photographs.

THE RAILWAY AGE IN BEDFORDSHIRE: Fred Cockman. Classic, illustrated acount of early railway history.

CHILTERN ARCHAEOLOGY: RECENT WORK:
A Handbook for the Next Decade: edited by Robin Holgate.
The latest views, results and excavations by twenty-three leading archaeologists throughout the Chilterns.

WHIPSNADE WILD ANIMAL PARK: 'MY AFRICA': Lucy Pendar.
Foreword by Andrew Forbes. Introduction by Gerald Durrell.
Inside story of sixty years of the Park's animals and people – full of anecdotes, photographs and drawings.

BOURNE and BRED:
A Dunstable Boyhood Between the Wars: Colin Bourne.
An elegantly written, well-illustrated book capturing the spirit of the town over fifty years ago.

ROYAL HOUGHTON: Pat Lovering.
Illustrated history of Houghton Regis from the earliest times to the present.

BEDFORDSHIRE'S YESTERYEARS Vol. 1:
The Family, Childhood and Schooldays:
Brenda Fraser-Newstead.
Unusual early 20th century reminiscences, with private photographs.

BEDFORDSHIRE'S YESTERYEARS Vol. 2:
The Rural Scene: Brenda Fraser-Newstead.
Vivid first-hand accounts of country life two or three generations ago.

BEDFORDSHIRE'S YESTERYEARS Vol. 3:
Craftsmen and Trades People:
Brenda Fraser-Newstead.
Fascinating recollections over several generations practising many vanishing crafts and trades.

BEDFORDSHIRE'S YESTERYEARS Vol. 4:
War Times and Civil Matters:
Brenda Fraser-Newstead.
Two World Wars, plus transport, law and order, etc.

THE CHANGING FACE OF LUTON: An Illustrated History:
Stephen Bunker, Robin Holgate and Marian Nichols.
Luton's development from earliest times to the present busy industrial town. Illustrated in colour and monochrome. The three authors from Luton Museum are all experts in local history, archaeology, crafts and social history.

THE MEN WHO WORE STRAW HELMETS:
Policing Luton, 1840–1974: Tom Madigan.
Meticulously chronicled history; dozens of rare photographs;
author served in Luton Police for nearly fifty years.

BETWEEN THE HILLS:
The Story of Lilley, a Chiltern Village: Roy Pinnock.
A priceless piece of our heritage – the rural beauty remains but
the customs and way of life described here have largely
disappeared.

GLEANINGS REVISITED:
Nostalgic Thoughts of a Bedfordshire's Farmer's Boy:
E W O'Dell.
His own sketches and early photographs adorn this lively
account of rural Bedfordshire in days gone by.

FARM OF MY CHILDHOOD, 1925–1947: Mary Roberts.
An almost vanished lifestyle on a remote farm near Flitwick.

THE VALE OF THE NIGHTINGALE:
The True Story of a Harpenden Family: Molly Andrews.
Victorian times to the present day in this lovely village.

THE TALL HITCHIN SERGEANT:
A Victorian Crime Novel based on fact:
Edgar Newman.
Mixes real police officers and authentic background with an
exciting storyline.

THE TALL HITCHIN INSPECTOR'S CASEBOOK:
A Victorian Crime Novel based on fact:
Edgar Newman.
Worthies of the time encounter more archetypal villains.

LEAFING THROUGH LITERATURE: Writer's Lives
in Hertfordshire and Bedfordshire:
David Carroll.
Illustrated short biographies of many famous authors and their
connections with these counties.

THE HILL OF THE MARTYR: An Architectural History
of St. Albans Abbey: Eileen Roberts.
Scholarly and readable chronological narrative history of
Hertfordshire and Bedfordshire's famous cathedral. Fully
illustrated with photographs and plans.

SPECIALLY FOR CHILDREN

VILLA BELOW THE KNOLLS:
A Story of Roman Britain:
Michael Dundrow.
An exciting adventure for young John in Totternhoe and Dunstable two thousand years ago.

ADVENTURE ON THE KNOLLS:
A Story of Iron Age Britain:
Michael Dundrow.
Excitement on Totternhoe Knolls as ten-year-old John finds himself back in those dangerous times, confronting Julius Caesar and his army.

THE RAVENS:
One Boy Against the Might of Rome:
James Dyer.
On the Barton Hills and in the south-east of England as the men of the great fort of Ravensburgh (near Hexton) confront the invaders.

Further titles are in preparation.
All the above are available via any bookshop, or from the publisher and bookseller

THE BOOK CASTLE
12 Church Street, Dunstable Bedfordshire, LU5 4RU
Tel: (01582) 605670